PRAISE FOR
HE MAKES ALL THINGS BEAUTIFUL

"For the past few years, I have had the amazing honor to sit at the feet at one of God's treasures, Marvita Franklin. She is one of those rare teaching jewels who comes along once in a lifetime and who God has gifted to bring Scriptures to life with realness and humor. Not only is Marvita anointed to teach, but God has also gifted her to encourage others to chase the dreams God planted within them. The book you hold in your hands will change your life if you allow the words to bathe your soul with its truths. Every page is filled with something that can be pondered and applied to make your life more pleasing to Abba Father. May you be *inspired*, *encouraged* and *transformed* as you read the riches in *He Makes All Things Beautiful*. I also hope you laugh as much as I do when I sit at her feet every Sunday morning. Marvita really is one in a million and chases God's heart like no other! Enjoy the ride!"

Debbie Dixon Barney
Operations Director
South Carolina School of Leadership

He Makes All Things Beautiful

God's transformation of our emotional
wounds, scars, and brokenness

MARVITA FRANKLIN

WESTBOW
PRESS
A DIVISION OF THOMAS NELSON

Scripture quotations marked "ESV" are taken from The Holy Bible: English Standard Version. Copyright © 2000; 2001 by Crossway Bibles, a division of Good News Publishers. Used by permission. All rights reserved.

Scripture quotations marked "HCSB" taken from The Holy Bible: Holman Christian Standard Version. Copyright 2009. Holman Bible Publishers. Used by permission.

Scripture quotations marked "NASB" taken from the New American Standard Bible®, Copyright © 1960, 1962, 1963, 1968, 1971, 1972, 1973, 1975, 1977, 1995 by The Lockman Foundation. Used by permission."

Scripture quotations marked "NIV" taken from The Holy Bible: New International Version ®. NIV®. Copyright © 1973, 1978, 1984 by International Bible Society. Used by permission of Zondervan. All rights reserved.

Scripture quotations marked "MSG" taken from The Message. Copyright © Eugene H. Peterson 1993, 1994, 1995, 1996, 2000, 2001, 2002. Used by permission of NavPress Publishing Group.

WestBow Press books may be ordered through booksellers or by contacting:

WestBow Press
A Division of Thomas Nelson
1663 Liberty Drive
Bloomington, IN 47403
www.westbowpress.com
1-(866) 928-1240

Because of the dynamic nature of the Internet, any web addresses or links contained in this book may have changed since publication and may no longer be valid. The views expressed in this work are solely those of the author and do not necessarily reflect the views of the publisher, and the publisher hereby disclaims any responsibility for them.

Any people depicted in stock imagery provided by Thinkstock are models, and such images are being used for illustrative purposes only.

Certain stock imagery © Thinkstock.

ISBN: 978-1-4497-9819-2 (sc)
ISBN: 978-1-4497-9820-8 (hc)
ISBN: 978-1-4497-9818-5 (e)

Library of Congress Control Number: 2013910740

Printed in the United States of America.

WestBow Press rev. date: 06/28/2013

To Tracy, Joshua, and Shannon

Because the legacy I hope to leave you is a passion
for God and an abiding love for His Word

In Memoriam

Chaplain Herrie L. Reed, Jr, LT Col, USAF
August 18, 1956-September 22, 2006

For encouraging in me a love for God's Word,
a passion to share it with others and for passing on the mantle
of leadership. You are remembered well and deeply missed.

THE JEWELS IN MY LIFE

I had a dream one morning as I was sleeping in my bed
I saw jewels of various colors as they danced inside my head
And from the Lord I heard a Word especially for me
A word that literally opened up a new reality

He said, "For where your treasure is, there your heart will be."
At once, I understood why He was saying this to me
The *jewels in my life*—the things of greatest worth
Did not consist of tangible stuff or things from on the earth

They were instead the people who had spoken into me
The rich "Words of life," which helped to shape my destiny
As I pondered all the more, I remembered what you'd done
How you prayed for me and loved me during the times I felt alone

The picture became clearer as I listened to His voice
Your "calling and election" were certainly by His choice
As iron sharpens iron, so you've helped to hone my skills
And encouraged me to press toward the mark and do the Father's will

You're the people who've inspired—you've encouraged me to soar
You're the people who have cried with me
Through each trial and closing door
Your name is written in my heart because into my life you've sown
Because of your faith and courage, it is by leaps and bounds I've grown

I will never be able to repay you for all of your sacrifice
For your guidance, your selflessness, and pouring out your life
So this poem is a small token of my love and gratitude
A simple way of saying how much I truly value you

When I've done all I can—as mother, daughter, friend, and wife
The things I'll treasure most are you—*the jewels in my life*
©2001, M. Franklin

CONTENTS

FOREWORD

The single, young missionary associate strode confidently into her much-anticipated meeting with the elders of the church. She was, after all, well along her journey of raising final support and ready to take the Gospel to faraway lands of those who have never heard. Never could she have known that by stepping through that door her life would suddenly and unexpectedly be forever changed.

During a simple time of listening and waiting before the Lord, a word was sent from heaven through one of the elders. It was a word about old unhealed wounds and offenses of the past . . . a word that caused this young lady to face what she had long buried and hidden in the deepest recesses of her heart. Beyond this encounter, a new beginning, a journey toward healing, restoration and freedom followed.

So many of us are like this young lady—secretly wounded, carrying grief and bearing offense and the lies that support them. We somehow dismiss that He, who bore our griefs and carried our sorrows, wants us to live in the provision of this costly freedom.

I am grateful that Marvita has written about the Lord making all things beautiful. She courageously addresses issues about emotional and spiritual wounds. She uncovers deadly mindsets and their toxic effect in the realm of our thinking.

Her book goes beyond an appeal to reasoning and good principles; it is solidly scriptural from cover to cover. Marvita not only reflects on stories of individuals within the Bible, but she looks at their motives, mindsets and the decisions that ultimately defined their destinies. Marvita understands that power to transform and liberate us comes from the Word. From Old Testament to New, she helps the reader uncover and apply the timeless truths from these accounts to his or her life.

Marvita's life is a picture of the tree in Psalm Chapter one. Her roots go deep beside the river, as one who both delights and meditates in the law of the Lord day and night. You, as the reader, will glean from the fruit of her life. May the transformational impact of this book come alive within you so that you, too, can proclaim, "He really does make all things beautiful."

Glenn Burchett
Executive Associate Pastor
Christian Life Church

PREFACE

In the spring of 2007, Angela Smith, women's ministry director for Christian Life Church, Columbia SC invited me to be one of several group breakout leaders for our annual women's retreat. The event was held at The Cove in Asheville, NC. That invitation began a relationship that has been a blessing and encouragement over the past six years. Her encouragement to me to be *God's girl for the moment* was instrumental in the development of this book.

Following the retreat, the Lord began speaking to my heart that another invitation would follow. In August 2007, it was Angela (again) who extended that invitation. This time, I would be the keynote speaker for a retreat in the spring of 2008. The theme for the retreat was "Something Beautiful." Early on, the Lord began speaking to my heart regarding what to share with the women who would attend. As the leader of Christian Life's Women's Ministry, *Women-Connecting-Women*, Angela's vision centers on what will, first, connect women to God and, then, to each other. Her emphasis always highlights that we are *real women with real faith doing real life.*

This book is the follow-up to that season. It was a tremendous privilege for me to speak to the wonderful women who attended that weekend. In the weeks following, I felt impressed by the Lord to continue pondering and formatting the message for this book.

It has been five years. The insights from that season still resonate with me in this one. As I walk out my own brokenness before the Lord, I am grateful for the ways He heals my wounds, invades my world on a regular basis and provides the beauty secrets necessary for my ongoing transformation.

Thank you Angela for being a beautiful example of God's heart and for your encouragement to me. After all of these years, it is still a precious watershed moment in God's process of transforming me. Love you bunches . . . . *Marvita*

> Whoever brings blessing will be enriched, and one who waters will himself be watered. (Proverbs 11:25 ESV)

ACKNOWLEDGEMENTS

To *my parents, Morris and Delores Mungin,* thank you for always believing in and encouraging me. Your love and support have helped to make me feel beautiful even in my most awkward seasons. I love you both very much! *Mom, how could you not know . . . ?*

To my brothers *Tony, Chris, Jason and your families* for being so loving and so much fun to be around. I love you all, and I am always refreshed by the time I spend with each of you.

To the *Jewels In My Life* who have come alongside me in every season of my life to continually remind me of how faithful God is and how really blessed I really am.

To *Rhonda Barnes* because having you as a BFF for the past 17 years has been one of the greatest outpourings of God's grace upon my life. Thank you for always reminding me of who I am in Christ.

To *Regina Wilson, Hope Valentine, Diana Raymond, Yolanda Martin, Reverend Carmen James, Caroline DeLeon, and Debbie Barney* because you are faithful, authentic and transparent friends. You always seem to be *on the ready* to warfare on my behalf and it ministers life to me.

To the Christian Life Church Leaders and your families, thank you for pouring out your lives in service to the Body of Christ.

To the best Sunday school class on the planet for your candor, authenticity and prayers. It's an honor to do "community" with you and to be "sharpened as iron sharpens iron."

To Debbie Blank for sharing and living what it means to "study to show thyself an approved workman."

INTRODUCTION

He has made everything beautiful in its time. He has also set eternity in the hearts of men; yet they cannot fathom what God has done from beginning to end. (Ecclesiastes 3:11 NIV *emphasis mine*)

He makes all things beautiful. In spite of our emotional wounds, scars or brokenness, God can transform us into something beautiful. The visual images before us everyday in fashion catalogs, department store displays and television ads send both blatant and subtle messages all of the time. Most of the time the message is *we aren't beautiful enough.* Our hips are too big, our busts are too small, our lips are too thin, or our hair is too short. Then there are the other messages: our skin is bad and our teeth are dull. If we believe all of the noise, we feel as though we're inadequate, don't have enough, don't do enough and can't be enough. Enough already!

The message of Scripture is very different: *God has made everything beautiful in its time*—including us, despite messages to the contrary. There is a beauty waiting to break forth from within us, a beauty that longs after who He is. It's a beauty that can only be accurately defined and understood within the framework of relationship with God through Christ.

The emphasis is on He

It is *God* who has made us beautiful! Whatever imperfections and unlovliness we've acquired along the way are transformed by His presence. God is the one doing this work in our lives. He is the one who transforms us. He is both able and willing to do it; however, we must be willing to embrace a more comprehensive definition of beauty. It means we stop allowing others to define beauty for us and reclaim the real beauty God intends for us.

We will need to take our cue from the apostle Paul and his lesson to the Corinthian Church—*it is foolishness to compare yourselves among yourselves (2 Corinthians 10:12)*. Paul was addressing the presumptions of a few people within the church. His physical appearance gave the impression he lacked what was necessary to hold them accountable. Paul cautioned his readers not to misunderstand his demeanor or physical presence as a lack of power or understanding. He made it clear that when man uses man as a measuring stick, every subsequent calculation is sure to be off. The same is true today. When we allow other people, cultural norms, or fashion trends to become the yardstick by which we measure our own worth or beauty, our calculations will be grossly skewed!

In comparing ourselves to others, we miss the unique beauty God has assigned to each of us. Our understanding is lacking when it becomes our goal to transform ourselves according to the standards of others. God has designed each of us to bear the image of who He is. Because we are so uniquely different, bearing His image must be about far more than our complexion, shape, muscle mass, or hair texture.

There is a much larger issue here. This is about *knowing* the God Who created the universe. He is intimately acquainted with every aspect of who we are. He understands every emotion we experience, and He deposited in us the very egos we often allow to become overblown. He has it in His power to transform all of our circumstances in a moment or over the course of time. This is about *knowing Him*. HE IS GOD. He is worthy of being known, pursued and loved just on the basis of His existence and what He has done in our lives. When we come to the place of appreciating the value of knowing Him because He wants to be known, it opens the door to true transformation and authentic beauty. So, what does this transformation look like?

> *Transformation occurs as you begin to see yourself as God sees you, say about yourself what God says and embrace the truth about you as He speaks it. Then, it won't matter what the naysayers think. It won't matter what color your skin is, what length or texture your hair is, or what size you are. That is the point at which you will begin hearing what He has been saying all along: "I AM the soundtrack of your life—and I AM the one who makes you beautiful."*

The road ahead

This book is organized into three parts. In Part 1, *He makes all things beautiful by healing our wounds.* I begin with emotional wounds because it's important to understand that our wounds don't repulse God, nor does He cringe at the sight of them. He is the One who really knows why they are there. He made a commitment a long time ago—*before the foundation of the world (Ephesians 1:4)*—to cause even our wounds and scars *to work together for good (Romans 8:28).* Though He's able to cause them to work together for good, He's also willing to heal our emotional wounds and give us beauty for ashes, the oil of joy for mourning and the garment of praise for the spirit of heaviness that occasionally plagues us. Why? It's His desire for us to be oaks of righteousness, the planting of the LORD, that He may be glorified. (Isaiah 61:3)

In Part 2, *He makes all things beautiful by invading our world.* We'll see situations where He invades an experience and invests Himself to transform people or situations into something beautiful. An important take away in this section is that God rarely does something in our lives that is solely about us. His invasion of our world brings with it the potential for a legacy of blessings in the lives of others as well. We will see Him put His finger on a life and witness the subsequent transformation that takes place. We will take note as He weaves together seemingly unconnected events to create a tapestry, which reflects His glory. That tapestry will cover the lives of many as they are drawn into relationship with Him.

In Part 3, *He makes all things beautiful by giving us beauty secrets for life.* This section highlights how we can encourage and nurture ourselves in the spa of His presence. It is here that authentic beauty is cultivated and matured. According to 2 Peter 1:3-9, God, by His divine power, has granted everything we need that pertains to whole and holy living. The *everything* He speaks of is accessed through *knowledge* of Him. The more intimate our knowledge of Him, the more we access and understand what is necessary to live out a *victorious Christian life.* It may not be a trial-free, conflict-free, or even drama-free life. However, we can live it from a victorious vantage point. It can still be a victorious Christian life.

As believers, it is both desirable and possible to live a victorious life amid the turmoil, struggle and challenges we face every day. The more intimately acquainted we are with Him the greater our awareness of the victory we have in Him. The details of our lives take on greater significance because they clearly communicate the day-to-day ways we overcome, and they also reveal the nature and character of the sovereign God who meets us where we are and *loves us to beautiful.*

Peter goes on to say that if the qualities we acquire as a result of *knowing* Him (intimacy) continue to grow and develop, we are poised and prepared to be both useful and fruitful. We will be strategically positioned to be beautiful and to be great as well. We will be great in the way God defines greatness. We will be available to love others and serve in the Kingdom of God. We will be available as ambassadors and friends. We will be available as Kingdom envoys to come alongside others in the ministry of reconciling others to Christ (2 Corinthians 5:18).

I pray you will be encouraged as you read these pages. Specifically, I pray you will abandon every mindset and attitude that has marred or jaded your belief about your own beauty. I pray you will embrace the vastness of God's everlasting love for you as well as the depth and extent of His grace toward you. Finally, I pray you will see yourself through the same filter through which He sees you: the selfless, atoning blood of our Lord Jesus Christ—who, though He committed no sin, became sin for us to make us the righteousness of God in Christ Jesus (2 Corinthians 5:21).

PART I

He Makes All Things Beautiful By Healing Our Wounds

We should begin by addressing our wounds. Many of us may not want to admit it, but we are *wounded*. Few of us want to believe our hurt goes very deep, but it does. Not only does our hurt run deep, it can also permeate every area of our lives. In many cases, we want so much to be pleasing to the Lord we're willing to live in a cloud of denial about the depth of our hurt. We want, in good faith, to be able to lift our hands and praise God in the midst of the storm. Don't get me wrong, we should certainly continue to *press on and praise through*. At the same time, however, we need to be honest with the Lord and ourselves about where we are emotionally and mentally. It's not as though He doesn't already know how wounded and broken we are. Hebrews 4:16 encourages us to draw near to the throne of grace with *confidence* to get the help we need. One translation says to come *boldly*. The words *confidence* and *boldly* literally mean *a freedom or frankness in speaking.*[1]

In other words when we approach the throne of grace, we need to be transparent and be authentic—it's our moment of truth. It is there at

His throne that we pour out our hearts before the Lord. We don't have to dress it up, reframe it, or dilute it. God wants us to share our stories in the raw. He wants us naked and unashamed before Him. The same issues that caused Adam and Eve to hide in the garden often put us on the run too. Guilt and shame cause us to withdraw from God's presence rather than run to Him. In the same way a sacrificial death provided clothing to cover their nakedness (Genesis 3:21), the sacrificial death of Christ and His shed blood covers (and atones) for our sin (Hebrews 9:22). Our shame and guilt are no longer obstacles that keep us from Him. Our willingness to be naked and open is an opportunity to draw near to Him and experience His healing and grace.

I

The Source of Our Wounds

God knows exactly where we've been hurt. He knows what emotional wounds remain and how severely we've been scarred. He understands our brokenness and the emptiness we feel. I have intentionally chosen a wound analogy because our woundedness is precisely one of the reasons Christ came to us. Isaiah 61:1 reminds us Christ was anointed to bring good news to those afflicted and bind up the brokenhearted—those who have been wounded emotionally and spiritually. Wounds can hinder and restrain us. Christ, however, came to set captives free and provide freedom through life in Him (Luke 4:18, 2 Corinthians 3:17).

Christ so understood the nature of our condition He willingly chose to experience His own wounding. His wounds, however, were for our transgressions. He bore the guilt and shame for our sin. He received the wages due for our disobedience. The death we deserved, He humbly accepted without complaint. Our punishment was laid on Him. In return, He provides healing to us (1 Peter 2:21-24).

The anatomy of physical wounds provides useful insight into how emotional and spiritual wounds impact our daily living. Let's begin with a common understanding of how wounds impact the physical body.

I'll be sensitive, so I won't make you queasy as I explain, but I think a few definitions will be helpful. Let's review how physical wounds and bedsores occur.

> Physical wounds occur when the *integrity of any tissue is compromised.* It may be caused by an act, by an infectious disease, or by an underlying condition. The types and causes of wounds are wide ranging. *Open wounds* take place when the skin has been compromised and underlying tissue is exposed. In a *closed wound,* the skin has not been compromised, but trauma to underlying structures has occurred. [2]

> Bedsores, more accurately called *pressure sores,* are areas of damaged skin and tissue that develop when *sustained pressure*—usually from a bed or wheelchair—*cuts off circulation to vulnerable parts of your body,* especially the skin on your buttocks, hips, and heels. *Without adequate blood flow, the affected tissue dies.*[3]

The previous explanation of wounds and bedsores provides a great description of how we sometimes get and stay emotionally wounded. In the case of offense, the integrity of a situation is compromised. As with a physical wound, it can be caused by the act of another, a sinful behavior, or our underlying suppositions. The impact can be wide ranging. In our lives, an *open wound* might take the form of some obvious hurt like a broken relationship or a violated trust. Our *closed wounds* may resemble unspoken hurts, betrayals, or disappointment. On the outside, we appear to be doing well. However, just beneath our surface, our hearts are broken or our psyches are damaged.

When an offense occurs, instead of working to resolve an issue or moving on (*turning*) we linger in one spot for too long. Bedsores can easily develop in places where no previous wound existed because pressure builds up and results in a sore. In a very similar way, staying on one thing—lingering too long on a betrayal, violation, or disappointment—can cause *spiritual and emotional bedsores* in us. An unwillingness to forgive a wrong or hurt can do serious damage. Some of us have acquired the sores because we couldn't turn ourselves. The injuries we had already sustained were so great we didn't have the strength (or understanding) to turn ourselves—change direction. In such cases, we often need others who love us to come alongside us to help. This represents increased blood flow in our lives—the sanctifying blood of Christ manifesting itself through the love of other believers coming alongside us.

Others of us have knowingly and willingly chosen to stay in one spot; this has allowed the wound to develop. We've rationalized that *we have the right* to stay in that spot because we have been wronged. Our staunch conviction to stay in that spot is intended to serve notice that *our rightness justifies our behavior.* As the pressure increases, redness (initial indication of an injury) develops and eventually there's a wound. Now, because we couldn't (or wouldn't) move on, forgive, or take a thought captive, we have to deal with more severe injuries—bitterness, anger, jealousy, envy, rebellion, pride, vindictive thoughts, or other emotions—which create more resistant strongholds in our lives.

There are other things or situations that may also appear to be the source of our wounds:

- misunderstandings between friends
- separation and divorce
- unexpected or unexplained illness
- unanswered questions about barrenness and infertility
- loss of a child
- betrayals, gossip and reprisals

- vengeance and unforgiveness
- unrealistic expectations of others
- hurtful and cutting words
- verbal or emotional abuse
- sexual or physical abuse/rape/sexual assault
- sexual immorality
- rejection from/by others
- neglect and abandonment
- abortion(s)
- judgment and criticism
- hope deferred and broken promises
- disobedience and bad behavior

The previous list isn't intended to be exhaustive. Each situation has within it some person or factor we perceive as the *culprit* responsible for our wound. These situations and a host of others like them may leave us feeling devastated, broken, victimized and, in some cases, emotionally traumatized. Many of the situations listed can spark emotionally charged discussions about very intimate and personal details of our lives. Though it's important to be sensitive to every difficult situation people may have encountered, it's also necessary to point out that these issues may only *appear* to cause our wounds. It is true other people, situations, or events can have a significant role in the wounding we experience. However, more often than most of us would care to admit, sometimes our wounds are *self-inflicted*. I wonder how many of our wounds are the result of our own poor choices and occur because we ignore a very practical and powerful concept of God's truth.

> Those who love Your law have great peace, and nothing causes them to stumble. (Psalm 119:165 NASB)

Yet that is exactly what is happening to many of us; we're *stumbling*. We are falling over things that get in our way. Even when we can see those things far off, we still manage, somehow, to run right into them and sustain some spiritual or emotional injury. The word *stumble* comes from two words that characterize faltering or falling over an obstacle.[4] However, the Psalmist suggests that when we have and maintain a love for God's Law—*His Word*—we can avoid those obstacles. To be clear, this isn't some magic formula. The entire context of Psalm 119 has to do with making God's Word a priority in our lives. When we do, we subsequently meditate on it for the benefit of intimacy with God, godly living and sustained peace. Psalm 1 reiterates the point by highlighting the benefits of meditating on, musing over and reflecting on God's Word. The Psalmist notes that, in the end, one man lives a life characterized by steadfastness and thriving in God's Word. It is a life in stark contrast to the man whose life is blown about like chaff and loose dirt. It is similar to the apostle Paul's encouragement in Ephesians 4:14 to not be tossed about with every wind of doctrine that crosses our path. The Word of God provides the grounding, focus and stability we need to live victorious lives in His presence *even when our circumstances fail us.*

We can avoid faltering and tripping over the things that would cause us to wound ourselves. What I'm suggesting is that many of us are wounded because we're *offended*. Offense is the trap we have fallen in, and it has contributed to our spiritual and emotional wounds. Even now, some of you reading these words may be offended. Why? Most of us want to believe we are above it—we're too emotionally mature to be offended by the *things* that happen to us. However, most of us also tend to embrace only the contemporary definition of *offense* instead of focusing on its biblical definitions.

In examining both the Old and New Testament uses of the word *offense*, the word has at its core the concept of being ensnared or trapped.[5]

In our contemporary understanding of the word, most of us don't envision an offense being a snare or trap. However, it is a very accurate description of what occurs when we are offended. It causes us to stumble and fall emotionally and spiritually. In the end, it isn't what someone else did or didn't do to us or will or won't do that is the problem. The central issue revolves around what *our reaction* will be and whether we will be ensnared by our own choices in the moment.

> He replied to them, "Go and report to John the things you have seen and heard: The blind receive their sight, the lame walk, those with skin diseases are healed, the deaf hear, the dead are raised, and the poor are told the good news. *And anyone who is not offended because of Me is blessed."*[6] (Luke 7:22-23 HCSB)

> When Jesus had finished these parables, he moved on from there. Coming to his hometown, he began teaching the people in their synagogue, and they were amazed. "Where did this man get this wisdom and these miraculous powers?" they asked. "Isn't this the carpenter's son? Isn't his mother's name Mary, and aren't his brothers James, Joseph, Simon and Judas? Aren't all his sisters with us? Where then did this man get all these things?" *And they took offense at him.* But Jesus said to them, "Only in his hometown and in his own house is a prophet without honor." And he did not do many miracles there because of their lack of faith.[7] (Matthew 13:57 NIV)

> When many of his disciples heard it, they said, "This is a hard saying; who can listen to it?" But Jesus, knowing in himself that his disciples were grumbling about this, said to them, *"Do you take offense at this?"*[8] (John 6:61 ESV)

John's disciples came to ask if Jesus was the Messiah for whom they had been waiting. Jesus sent word to John regarding the miracles that took place. That was His response to John's question. He then said "*blessed is he who is not offended in Me.*" His response had everything to do with *what He did* as well as what people *thought of what He did* and Who He was. The Greek word *skandalizo*[9] used in these passages is a derivative of the word *skandalon.*[10] Skandalon refers to the trigger of the trap on which bait is placed. In each of the encounters referenced, the listeners had a choice. They could choose to believe Jesus was the fulfillment of the truths spoken through prophets and angels or they could abandon those truths, move in their own direction, and fall into a trap. It seems then *unbelief* would be at least one trigger that could provoke offense.

In Luke 7:23, unbelief—despite all of the miracles they had heard of and witnessed—would have caused them to fall into the trap. In Matthew 13:57, unbelief rears its head again as the trigger that sets off the trap of offense. In this case, they refused to perceive Jesus as anything other than a carpenter's son. In John 6:61, the disciples had a difficult time fathoming the concept of drinking His blood and eating His flesh. It was difficult because they may have understood their thinking had to change—it would require a paradigm shift. They would be acknowledging Christ as the acceptable sacrifice for sin—the Lamb of God who really would take away the sin of the world.

Every time the invitation to be offended presents itself, we are being led down a treacherous path. The path ends in the *trap of offense.* It is paved with unbelief, rationalization, justification and supposed rightness. Each signpost and intersection assures us we've earned the right to be on this road because of the wrong we've been dealt. It's essential to remember, however, the one conducting us on this journey has been a liar since the beginning. Scripture tells us he is the Father of

Lies (John 8:44). Satan wants us to justify our bad behavior. It provides more information for him to use to accuse us before our Heavenly Father (Revelation 12:10). So, before we get things twisted, let's tackle the real source of our wounds.

Offense is a major contributor to our wounds.

We find ourselves wounded when someone behaves badly toward us, or someone says something negative about us. We believe we're wounded because of their behavior. However, it's very likely we may be reacting emotionally to *our own thoughts* about what was said or done. *Often our thoughts about the situation have little to do with what actually occurred.* We are wounded when someone overlooked something we thought should have been important to him or her. We convince ourselves *their actions* are the root causes of our problem. It is true the actions of others may contribute to the root system of the toxic atmosphere we're experiencing. However, there is an original taproot[11] that gives life to what is really going on. *The taproot is offense.* In choosing offense—choosing to step, fall, or jump into the trap—we've opted to entertain unproductive thoughts that don't add value to our lives.

Much of my work experience is in the realm of leader development and coaching. It began during the second half of my Air Force career and continued after I retired. A few years ago, I read a book, which I think highlights a pattern of behavior that frames the consequences of offense. In their book, *Crucial Conversations*, Kerry Patterson (et al.) characterize the process very simply. First, we see or hear something. Then, we think something about what we saw or heard. We subsequently react emotionally not to what took place but to *our own thoughts about what took place.* Finally, we take action. Most of the time, we are reacting to what we *feel* about *our own thoughts,* not what actually occurred.[12]

If Patterson and his friends are correct, then we are more responsible than anyone else for the *road trip* our minds are taking us on. Frankly, this shouldn't surprise us. Both Old and New Testament writings remind us of the need to manage our thought processes. Don't misunderstand where I'm headed with this. Bad things happen. Malicious people sometimes do ugly and evil things. The people we love may make poor choices that impact us in significant and devastating ways. We live in a fallen and imperfect world (Genesis 3). Despite all of that *we are still responsible for our responses* to the things occurring within and around us.

Remember God's warning to Cain after he was *offended* by God's response to Abel's better offering? God warned Cain that sin was crouching at the door and its desire was for him (Genesis 4:7). In short, sin was awaiting the opportunity for Cain to invite it in. In his case, offense would be the envelope through which he would receive the invitation to sin. Cain didn't get permission to *pass the buck* to anyone else. It was Cain's responsibility to master, subdue and take authority over the power of sin that wanted control over him. Neither do we have permission to pass the buck to anyone else. The buck stops with us, and we stop at Christ!

It is Christ Who died so that sin and death would no longer have power (mastery) over us (Hebrews 2:14-15). It is Christ Who died in order for us to draw near to God. Christ died so that we might live *victoriously* in the presence of God. He knows we are hurt and that we feel betrayed. He instructs us to humble ourselves under His almighty hand and cast our cares upon Him *because* He cares for us (1 Peter 5:6-7). To do so, we must first take ownership of what ails us. I can't *cast my cares* on Him if I keep pretending I don't have any. I can't cast the feelings associated with my wounds and hurts on Him if I'm in denial regarding their existence. I can't expect to truly deal with the issues impacting my life if I continue to blame others for them.

If the story I tell myself is that it is someone else's fault, then I will always have an excuse for why *I* don't need to change. If the story I tell myself is that I am a victim of circumstances—my history, my situation, or my wounds—I may never take ownership of my own feelings, actions and life choices.

Our own uncontrolled thoughts are most often the catalyst for our bad behavior. Uncontrolled thoughts ultimately create traps for us. Uncontrolled thoughts can have destructive power with the force of a *juggernaut*. The Bible is full of examples of people who were ensnared by the trap of uncontrolled thoughts. They behaved badly because they chose to be offended—ensnared and trapped—when things didn't go their way. They couldn't control, direct, or manipulate the behavior of others or circumstances to work in their favor. They couldn't *manage the perceptions* others had of them. Because they couldn't *control others or circumstances* around them, their thinking was sometimes distorted, their thoughts ran rampant and bad behavior ensued.

> Now I, Paul, myself urge you by the meekness and gentleness of Christ—I who am meek when face to face with you, but bold toward you when absent! I ask that when I am present I need not be bold with the confidence with which I propose to be courageous against some, who regard us as if we walked according to the flesh. For though we walk in the flesh, we do not war according to the flesh, for the weapons of our warfare are not of the flesh, but divinely powerful for the destruction of fortresses. We are destroying speculations and every lofty thing raised up against the knowledge of God, and we are *taking every thought captive to the obedience of Christ*, and we are ready to punish all disobedience, whenever your obedience is complete. (2 Corinthians 10:1-6 NASB, *emphasis mine*)

The apostle Paul warns us to take every thought captive to the obedience of Christ. We are to *wrestle our thoughts to the ground* and *make them bow in submission* to the truth of God's Word. When our thoughts attempt to convince us that the person we've committed to sharing our life with is unworthy of love, we need to get our wrestling clothes on. When we attempt to convince ourselves that our selfish desires are more important than what is right or lawful, we must be prepared to put a knee on the neck of *speculation* and make it bow in submission. When we buy into the lie *God doesn't understand what it takes to live in the real world and His truths for life are outdated*, we need to smack down the *lofty thing* and send it back to where it came from.

The sooner we recognize the real source of our wounds, the better equipped we will be to embrace strategies to keep offense from taking root in our lives.

2

When Offense Takes Root

Offense can be deadly! I hope that's clear. In case it isn't, let's examine some accounts from Scripture where offense got the best of a few people. In *most* cases, these are people who seemed to genuinely love God though there are a few exceptions. These examples represent those times when they didn't take their thoughts captive. Instead they allowed their speculations, rationalizations and unbelief to create pits and traps for them.

Saul chose offense when the people praised David's exploits

So David went out wherever Saul sent him, and prospered; and Saul set him over the men of war. And it was pleasing in the sight of all the people and also in the sight of Saul's servants. It happened as they were coming, when David returned from killing the Philistine, that the women came out of all the cities of Israel, singing and dancing, to meet King Saul, with tambourines, with joy and with musical instruments. *The women sang as they played, and said, " Saul has slain his thousands, and David his ten thousands."* Then Saul became very angry, for this saying displeased him; and he said, "They have ascribed to David ten thousands, but to me they have ascribed thousands. Now what more can he have but the kingdom?" *Saul looked at David with suspicion from that day on.* (1 Sam 18:5-9 NASB *emphasis mine*)

The story Saul told himself was one that focused on comparison. Unfortunately he came up short. Imagine you're Saul. You are the King of Israel and *sovereignly anointed and appointed by God* to lead His people (1 Samuel 9:15-17, 10:1). You stand head and shoulders above most men. You're not perfect, but who is? Then along comes a young shepherd who has also been *anointed by God* to replace you. The people adore him to the point of honoring him above you! Yes, that's enough to start the *juggernaut* moving.

Saul was offended—ensnared—not only by his view of David's popularity but his own apparent fall from grace as well. Saul was the King and a warrior. It was David, however, whose courage and character commanded the attention of the people and received their praise. Saul focused on what the people said and put his eyes on David. From Saul's perspective, David's success had disrupted the *perceptions* the people had of Saul. He perceived David was taking something from him—usurping honor and glory Saul felt he deserved. He was angry because he couldn't control the outcome of what was taking place. He began telling himself a very negative story. He also set himself up in comparison to David. Saul saw what David had done to Goliath, knew he was a valiant warrior and the Lord was with him. Instead of celebrating the young warrior's accomplishments, he compared himself to him. He made a major mistake that typically results in offense.

Saul heard the women's praise, told himself a story about what he heard, had an emotional response to that story and his bad behavior followed.[13] From there, the *juggernaut* gained momentum: *"Now what more can he have but the kingdom?"* It went from David being lauded by the local ladies for his valiant accomplishments to accusations of attempting to usurp Saul's authority and take over his kingdom. From that point on, Saul looked at him suspiciously. That suspicion contributed to Saul's negative story and attitude toward David. Saul's offense opened him up to evil influences and bad behaviors. We even see Saul hurling a spear at David because of his thoughts (1 Samuel 18:10). As Saul's negative thoughts gained momentum, he began behaving badly. His negative thoughts and bad behavior gave way to fear and dread (1 Samuel 18:12). Saul was unable to manage the perceptions of others. He had heard other people praising David, compared himself to David and became frustrated and wounded in the process. The remainder of his life would be characterized by this frustration and pain from a *self-inflicted wound.*

Saul's comparison of himself to David certainly seems to have created the snare into which he fell. It was also the cause of his subsequent wound. In 1 Samuel 15:28 God tells Saul the kingdom will pass to someone better than him—Saul's comparisons were futile. While it will later become apparent David has his own shortcomings, *David's anointing and successes were not the cause of Saul's wounds.* Saul's own choices served as the catalyst for the wounds he carried with him. This highlights an important life lesson: The blessings bestowed on another person's life are never the source or cause of our personal drama.

This wasn't the first time we could see Saul being overly concerned with what others thought. He faced the same dilemma twice before. The first time was when he made an oath to kill anyone who ate before the evening while he was still avenging his enemies (1 Samuel 14:24). His son, Jonathan, knew nothing of the oath. Jonathan ate a bit of honey to refresh himself while trekking through the hill country of Ephraim with soldiers. When Saul later discovered what Jonathan had done, he was prepared to put him to death. However, the people convinced Saul it was inappropriate on the basis of the great deliverance Jonathan had facilitated for Israel. In short, Saul broke the oath on basis of what the people wanted. Now, in fairness to Saul, I can't imagine any parent being eager to slay his or her own child for the sake of an oath. My point here, however, is the pattern we see in Saul's life of allowing what others thought of him to be the motive for his choices and decisions.

In 1 Samuel 15 Saul is commanded to utterly destroy the Amalekites (people, property and all animals) because of their sins against Israel. Saul disobeys and spares the animals as well as their King, Agag. When confronted by Samuel about his disobedience, Saul *disconnects himself* from what was clearly a violation of the commandment God gave him:

> Saul said, "*They* have brought them from the Amalekites, for the people spared the best of the sheep and of the oxen to sacrifice to the Lord your God, and the rest *we* have devoted to destruction." (1 Samuel 15:15 ESV *emphasis mine*)

He included himself, however, when pointing out the behaviors that were in compliance with the command. He goes on to inform Samuel that *because he feared the people, he listened to their voice* (1 Samuel 15:21,24). Saul allowed what others thought and desired to influence his thinking and behavior before the Lord. He was unwilling to take responsibility for and ownership of his actions as King. God's command was clear, " . . . utterly destroy . . . ." Saul, however, disobeyed because it was more pleasing to the people to keep the cattle for sacrificial offerings.

Miriam chose offense regarding Moses' marriage to a Cushite wife

> Miriam and Aaron spoke against Moses because of the Cushite woman whom he had married, for he had married a Cushite woman. And they said, *"Has the LORD indeed spoken only through Moses? Has he not spoken through us also?"* And the LORD heard it. Now the man Moses was very meek, more than all people who were on the face of the earth. And suddenly the LORD said to Moses and to Aaron and Miriam, "Come out, you three, to the tent of meeting." And the three of them came out. And the LORD came down in a pillar of cloud and stood at the entrance of the tent and called Aaron and Miriam, and they both came forward. And he said, "Hear my words: If there is a prophet among you, I the LORD make myself known to him in a vision; I speak with him in a dream. Not so with my servant Moses. He is faithful in all my house. With him I speak mouth to mouth, clearly, and not in riddles, and he beholds the form of the LORD. *Why then were you not afraid to speak against my servant Moses?"* (Numbers 12:1-8 ESV, *emphasis mine*)

Miriam let offense take her too far. She *stumbled* over Moses' Cushite wife. Her thoughts about Moses' wife created the trap into which she fell. Scripture doesn't reveal much about Moses' Cushite wife. We don't know (for sure) if she was, in fact, Zipporah from Exodus 2:21, or another woman. Whoever she was, Miriam wasn't happy. Whether the issue was *racial* (the Cushites descended from Ham, Noah's son who dishonored him[14]), or *relational* (she just didn't like her) makes no difference. Whatever the reason, it became a trap for Miriam and the catalyst for her wounding. Her own thoughts about the matter provoked her bad behavior and were responsible for the subsequent consequences.

Here again, the issue of comparison comes into play. From Aaron and Miriam's perspective, God spoke mightily through them as well. The implication from Scripture is they assumed they were equal in status to Moses with regard to their calling and leadership roles in Israel—clearly they were incorrect. God's call and anointing on Moses was specific to who Moses was *and* how the Lord intended to use Moses' life for His own glory.

Miriam and Aaron may have viewed being used by God as something attributable to their own abilities and identity. The very statement they make in verse 2 may indicate a lack of humility regarding their call. A deep humility, however, characterized Moses' calling and the intimacy he shared with God. It is God who points out that Moses was the most humble man on the face of the earth (Numbers 12:3). This may also be evidenced by his lack of response to Aaron and Miriam's carping. In the end, it would be God who had the last word on the matter.

While it seems her offense was rooted in her problem with Moses' wife, what Miriam actually spoke against was the anointing and call God had placed on Moses' life. Her error was costly. God didn't just call her out—He called her out in a way that was apparent to everyone. First, God corrected her and Aaron's misunderstanding of Moses' relationship with Him. This is interesting because we often fall into the snare of offense because we lack a real understanding of God's motive, character and nature. He doesn't need our permission to move or act in someone's life or on his or her behalf.

Miriam's offense *distorted her perception* of God's sovereignty in choosing Moses and interacting with him in a special way. The Cushite wife was merely the point of reference Miriam used to justify her own bad behavior. God clarified that He didn't just speak through Moses

(Numbers 12:6-8), but He spoke to Moses mouth-to-mouth (ESV). Apparently, Miriam knew this because God questions why that fact alone didn't deter her from speaking against Moses (Numbers 12:8). Again, it may be her offense clouded her judgment. This is often the case. When offense distorts our perception or clouds our judgment, it causes the significant to diminish and the insignificant to become grossly overrated or enlarged.

In Miriam and Aaron's case, God's anger burned against them. Although both Moses and Aaron do intercede for her, she must still bear the consequences of her error. Even Moses' response (or the lack thereof) exemplifies and foreshadows the powerful New Testament principle of entrusting ourselves to the righteous Judge. Despite railings, mocking and evil targeted toward Him, Jesus refused to render the same in return. He, instead, entrusted Himself to the righteous Judge (1 Peter 2:21-23). Moses, too, allowed the *Righteous Judge* to do the talking and settle the issue. Moses, again, assumes the role of intercessor to plead for mercy on Miriam's behalf. Here again is a beautiful picture for us as well. Today, Christ lives at the right hand of God doing the same for us continually (Hebrews 7:25).

Lastly, though it appears Miriam was forgiven of her sin of speaking against Moses and was subsequently healed, we never hear of her dancing and prophesying in the presence of the Lord again. Perhaps she did and no record of it is made. At the same time, I wonder if her *choice* to allow offense to enter in cost a much higher price than seven days of leprosy. Thank God for the blood of Jesus! The Scripture makes it clear that because we've been justified by Christ's death on the cross, we have peace with God (Romans 5:3). Though we make mistakes and falter in our interactions with God and others, Christ's blood cleanses us of sins as we confess them and seek His forgiveness. His Word will continually wash us as we meditate on it day and night.

David chose offense when Nabal snubbed him and dismissed his benevolence

> And Nabal answered David's servants, "Who is David? Who is the son of Jesse? There are many servants these days who are breaking away from their masters. Shall I take my bread and my water and my meat that I have killed for my shearers and give it to men who come from I do not know where?" So David's young men turned away and came back and told him all this. And David said to his men, "Every man strap on his sword!" And every man of them strapped on his sword. David also strapped on his sword. And about four hundred men went up after David, while two hundred remained with the baggage. (1 Samuel 25:10-13 ESV)

> Now David had said, "Surely in vain have I guarded all that this fellow has in the wilderness, so that nothing was missed of all that belonged to him, and he has returned me evil for good. God do so to the enemies of David and more also, if by morning I leave so much as one male of all who belong to him." (1 Samuel 25:21-22 ESV)

This time, it was David who stumbled over Nabal's disregard for who he was and the benevolent protection he had provided to Nabal while watching his field. What exactly did Nabal do? David and his men had protected Nabal's property and servants. When David highlights that fact in hope of gaining provision for his men, Nabal completely disregarded both the act and David as well. In doing so, he scorned David's favor, protection and reputation. While it is true Nabal's actions were intended to spurn David, it was David who had *power* over his own response to those actions.

Pay attention to *the story David told himself* as the events unfolded. David said, *"He has returned to me evil for good."* David heard Nabal's response to his request and *thought* his actions were evil against him. This was the negative story David told himself. He was unable to *manage the perceptions* Nabal had of him. *Didn't Nabal know that David was God's anointed?* As the *juggernaut* of his negative thoughts gained momentum, David convinced himself the only sensible solution was to kill every male among Nabal's household as a means of avenging himself. Here again is the pattern: we see or hear something, we tell ourselves a story, we respond emotionally and we act on our story.[15] It is worth noting that we later find out from his wife, Abigail, Nabal's name means *fool*. Despite this, David was still responsible for how *he* would respond.

It was Abigail's intercession and mediation that prevented David's offense from escalating. Her intervention is a beautiful picture of how we, too, can come alongside people and assist in this area. Abigail helps David redirect his thinking regarding the matter. She reminds him of God's promises to him regarding his rule over Israel. She also points out that David would regret having shed Nabal's blood for no cause. Abigail's note that the bloodshed would have been without cause highlights that Nabal's actions fall into the realm of *the insignificant being grossly overrated*. In this case, perhaps David was too focused on himself. His own actions were the real catalyst for the trap that could have impacted his ascension to King.

Naaman chose offense when Elisha sent him to bathe in a river to cure his leprosy

> Naaman, commander of the army of the king of Syria, was a
> great man with his master and in high favor, because by him

the LORD had given victory to Syria. He was a mighty man of valor, but he was a leper. (2 Kings 5:1 ESV)

So Naaman came with his horses and chariots and stood at the door of Elisha's house. And Elisha sent a messenger to him, saying, "Go and wash in the Jordan seven times, and your flesh shall be restored, and you shall be clean." But Naaman was angry and went away, saying, "Behold, I thought that he would surely come out to me and stand and call upon the name of the LORD his God, and wave his hand over the place and cure the leper. (2 Kings 5:9-11 ESV)

Naaman was a man accustomed to being lauded and celebrated. He was a great man and highly respected. Perhaps, Naaman, like many of us, wanted a big display of God's power. He showed up on Elisha's doorstep with a huge entourage accompanying him. Maybe it wasn't only about the fact that Elisha's God was a Healer. Maybe, just maybe, Naaman also considered how his own notoriety might increase once this great display had taken place. Imagine how Naaman must have felt when Elisha's *servant* came to the door with instructions on what he needed to do. Elisha didn't even bother to meet him at the door after the long trip and huge caravan! He sent a messenger who told Naaman to go dip himself in a dirty river. Naaman couldn't *manage the perceptions* of Elisha. Naaman's military fame hadn't convinced Elisha he was important enough to come out and heal the military commander in some big, flashy display. Despite his physical affliction, Naaman's response hints at his own *sense of self-importance.* His real problem was that he simply wasn't able to convince Elisha of how important he was.

Now follow what happens. Naaman's *thoughts* become the source of his offense: "*I thought . . . he will come out to me . . . stand and call on*

the name of the Lord . . . wave his hand over the place and cure the leper."
Yes, Naaman was ready for something spectacular—maybe he was
used to spectacle and grandeur. Yet God's instructions were simple and
faith enabling. The only thing to be showed off on this day would be a
demonstration of God's sovereignty and power. If Naaman wanted to
be part of it obedience was the only valid response. Naaman's *thoughts*
about the situation caused his ire. Unable to manage Elisha or the
messenger's perception of who he was, he was frustrated and offended.
It was only after his own servants' counsel to him in verse 13, *" . . .
if he said . . . do something great,"* that Naaman's heart and thoughts
shifted. Once that happened, he was able to respond in obedience to the
Prophet's instruction and receive the healing for which he had come.

The interventions of Naaman's servants provide a great life lesson
for us. We sometimes need our friends to talk us off of a ledge. We need
them to help back us away from the cliff of doubt and unbelief. It is a
great blessing to have friends who possess the *courage* to say to us what
we need to hear in the right moments. Naaman was allowing his own
thought processes to get in the way of the amazing healing that awaited
him. All he needed to do was go dip himself in the river. Wouldn't
it have been ridiculous for him to miss out on his blessing because it
didn't arrive in the package he expected? Yet, we often make the same
mistake. We dismiss the validity and magnitude of a blessing because
it comes wrapped in packaging that isn't to our liking or doesn't meet
our expectations.

It's important to note that we don't see a lack of faith in Naaman's
response to his situation. He didn't doubt God's ability to heal him or
Elisha's role as God's prophet. In fact, in Luke 4:27, Jesus reproves His
townspeople because of their lack of faith. In doing so, He points out
that there were many in the region in Naaman's day who had leprosy,
yet only Naaman was healed. Naaman may have struggled with offense

and a slightly distorted sense of self-worth in this situation, but a lack of faith wasn't his problem.

Haman chose offense when Mordecai refused to bow to him

> After these things King Ahasuerus promoted Haman the Agagite, the son of Hammedatha, and advanced him and set his throne above all the officials who were with him. And all the king's servants who were at the king's gate bowed down and paid homage to Haman, for the king had so commanded concerning him. But Mordecai did not bow down or pay homage. Then the king's servants who were at the king's gate said to Mordecai, "Why do you transgress the king's command?" And when they spoke to him day after day and he would not listen to them, they told Haman, in order to see whether Mordecai's words would stand, for he had told them that he was a Jew. And when Haman saw that Mordecai did not bow down or pay homage to him, Haman was filled with fury. (Esther 3:1-5 ESV)

Wow . . . talk about a guy who may have taken himself way, too, seriously! Haman may be the epitome of what happens when we begin to take too seriously our own hype. His is an example of what happens when we waste needless energy on trying to *manage the perceptions* of others. He desperately tried to manage Mordecai's perception of how important he was. Mordecai knew better and refused to bow . . . even for comfort's sake. He knew there was only one true and living God who deserved his worship.

A central issue in Haman's distorted perception is that he thought Mordecai's refusal to bow in worship to him was about him as a person. Nothing could be further from the truth. Mordecai's refusal to bow was directly connected to the true object of his affection—the Lord God—Yahweh. Mordecai was Jew (ESV). As such, his commitment was to worship only God (Deuteronomy 6:4-9). Haman made it about Haman. He was furious when he *saw* Mordecai would not pay homage to him. In doing so, he further aggravated his *self-inflicted wound.*

I believe the King's edict to honor Mordecai represented an opportunity for Haman to repent—to turn from the bitterness of the offense and let it go. His own *arrogance* and *self-centeredness* kept him from doing so. He chose instead to linger in that place and intensify his wound.

Despite Haman's promotions and accolades from the King, he allowed himself to be consumed with the one thing he could not control—Mordecai's perception of him. To Mordecai, Haman was just another man. Though he may have deserved honor, he was not worthy of worship. Worship belongs to God alone. Ultimately, Haman's stumbling block was *his own over-estimation of who he was.*

It's also worth noting that it is the king's servants who stir up this pot of mess. They are the ones who told Haman of Mordecai's refusal to bow. Haman allowed the perceptions and opinions of others to shape his thoughts and fuel his reaction to those thoughts.

Haman couldn't manage Mordecai's perception of his significance. Although Scripture doesn't indicate how others in the crowd of people were responding when Mordecai refused to bow before Haman, it's likely that many of them did notice and their response may have contributed to how slighted Haman would have felt. Haman's expectation was that everyone would bow before him; he reveled in every moment of it. He must have been severely annoyed and angered by Mordecai's failure to render to him the homage he felt he was due. Haman's choice cost him dearly. Not only did he suffer, but his choices significantly impacted his family as well.

Esther, too, could have chosen offense knowing Haman's desire to destroy her people. She also could have chosen offense when Mordecai reminded her that her position as queen wouldn't protect her from any retribution intended toward the Jews. Instead, however, she chose to focus on the One who could truly deliver her people—Yahweh. The King (Ashausuerus) became an instrument of God's deliverance in the lives of the Jewish people.

I wonder how many of us, like Haman, would find ourselves offended when others don't consider us the *big deal* we suppose ourselves to be? We make an issue of something that, at its core, has nothing to do with us. A best friend makes a personal decision (without telling us) that is in the best interest of her own family, yet we take it personally because of the gap we may feel in our lives. A supervisor chooses another employee for a promotion because they are best qualified and will better serve the future direction of the company. We, however, make it about us and amplify our own feelings of rejection. A dear friend makes a decision not to confide in us while walking through a fiery trial. When we later find out about it, we tell ourselves that not sharing it with us was about us instead of honoring his right to privacy—even if the person is a close friend.

At the end of the day, most of us, probably, are not as important to those around us as we think we are. I am not talking about the genuine relationships we have with people who love and care for us. I am referring to the more random social acquaintances we tend to have. Many of us might find ourselves very disappointed to know that not as many people think about us as much as we think they do. The fact is, we may not be on as many radar screens as we presume we are. When they do pay attention, maybe we shouldn't put too much stock in it. I'm sure it's much more healthy to *lean into the opinion of God* rather than *stand on the opinions of man*. Haman's story is a tragic reminder of what happens when we fall victim to our own *distorted perceptions of ourselves* and an *over-inflated sense of self-importance*.

When offense takes root . . .

There *is* legitimate value in the emotion of anger; however, there is never any gain from choosing to be snared by offense. It steals any chance we have of experiencing peace—the absence of turmoil. When offense takes root, it can dramatically distort our opinion. Molehills become mountains and toothpicks become tree trunks. Offense takes our focus off of our own questionable behavior and magnifies the behavior of others. It sets us up to be critical and judgmental. It causes us to make poor and irrational choices in situations that require wisdom and clarity. Offense often causes us to over-inflate our own self-worth, and it may motivate us to seek vengeance against others.

The bottom line is this: our offense (to include the accompanying wounds and distortions) is usually the result of our own thoughts. It is the trap we set for ourselves even if someone else's actions were the catalyst for our thoughts. I'm not implying others shouldn't be held accountable for their actions. We also shouldn't minimize the wrong behavior others may engage in when it negatively impacts us. At the same time, the bad behavior of others will never serve as adequate justification for our own bad behavior. When we render evil for evil, offense for offense, or wound for wound it has lasting consequences. We will have to deal with those consequences at some point. We can find ourselves with a troubled heart, at odds with God and missing out on the intimacy of His presence.

I've mixed quite a few metaphors in addressing offense—tap roots, juggernauts, traps and snares. At the end of the day, the primary purpose is to highlight the destructive and toxic nature of offense as well as its residual effects. It is subtle in its devastation because there appears to be a valid *rightness* in identifying the *wrongness* of others toward us. The real tragedy of surrendering to its power is that *it deludes us into believing what we're doing isn't nearly as bad as what they did.*

3

Uprooting Offense

The previous chapter focused on a few people who *chose* to let offense get a foothold in their lives. In this chapter, we'll shift our focus to those in Scripture who appear to have made a strategic decision to uproot offense in its early stages. They chose not to be offended by their circumstances or the bad behavior of others. As we review their stories, we will see they didn't bother trying to manage the perceptions of others. They relied on God's faithfulness when they couldn't make sense of the circumstances. When they were *unable to connect the dots* of their situation, they remembered *their connection to Him* and to His promises.

Sarah . . . when traded for her husband's life

Now there was a famine in the land; so Abram went down to Egypt to sojourn there, for the famine was severe in the land. It came about when he came near to Egypt, that he said to Sarai his wife, "See now, I know that you are a beautiful woman; and when the Egyptians see you, they will say, 'This is his wife'; and they will kill me, but they will let you live. "Please say that you are my sister so that it may go well with

me because of you, and that I may live on account of you."
(Genesis 12:10-13 NASB)

> But the Lord struck Pharaoh and his house with great plagues
> because of Sarai, Abram's wife. Then Pharaoh called Abram
> and said, "What is this you have done to me? Why did you
> not tell me that she was your wife? "Why did you say, 'She is
> my sister,' so that I took her for my wife? Now then, here is
> your wife, take her and go." (Genesis 12:17-19 NASB)

Over the course of 24 years, Sarah had traveled from the home she knew with her husband along with a caravan of servants, herdsmen and maids. They were moving to a land God had promised to show Abram. Along the way, her beauty captivated those living in the nations surrounding them. Even at 65 years of age, she was so strikingly beautiful that her husband was sure he would be killed because of it (Genesis 12:12). The Pharaoh of Egypt found her so beautiful, he took her as his wife—and *her husband let him*. It was only after the Lord struck Pharaoh and his house with great plagues because of Sarai that he let her go (Genesis 12:17).

In Genesis 12:19, Pharaoh rebukes Abram because he deceived him. Abram allowed Pharaoh to take Sarai as his wife. It's difficult to tell if the implication is that Pharaoh may have been *physically intimate* with her. Whatever the case it must have been a harrowing experience for Sarai to be traded to a foreign king in order to spare the life of her husband. There may have been a sense of abandonment and betrayal. Maybe Abram didn't think they would take her. Perhaps, they both thought that saying she was his sister would get them safely through the region.

In addition to all of this she had not been able to give Abram a son. Sarai was barren. Because of her barrenness, she later came up with the questionable plan to allow her husband to sleep with one of her maids. The maid would bear a child for her (Genesis 16:2). It should be noted here that the Egyptian maid she gave to Abram was, in all likelihood, one of the female servants Pharaoh gave to Abram in payment for Sarai. So it seems that the problems that beset them when they fled to Egypt to avoid the famine, were still haunting them. This gift from Pharaoh would become a thorn in Sarai's side. Her plan was a disaster! Her maid, Hagar, did conceive a child with Abram. In turn, Hagar began to hate Sarai and treat her with contempt. Sarai blamed Abram for the debacle. His response was that Sarai should do whatever she pleased to deal with *her problem*. What a mess they had created. Yet in the midst of all of this mess, there is a *promise* on the table.

> Then they said to him, "Where is Sarah your wife?" And he said, "There, in the tent." He said, "I will surely return to you at this time next year; and behold, Sarah your wife will have a son." And Sarah was listening at the tent door, which was behind him. (Genesis 18:9-10 NASB)

In Genesis 18, three visitors approached the place where Abraham was living. It may not have occurred to Sarah (whose name was changed as part of the covenant) that the visitors would have anything to do with her personally. Abraham busied himself with preparing a meal for his guests while Sarah did what she needed to do to ensure it was a success. The Lord had come in response to the outcry rising from Sodom and Gomorrah. However, before He would go there, He had a word for Abraham.

Ishmael, Abraham and Hagar's son, was 13 years old. I wonder if Abraham thought much more about the promise that his heir would come from Sarah's womb. Sarah, too, may have accepted that the son born of the maid who despised her might be the only son she would ever have. She was 89 years old—past childbearing age. That's an indication that she was probably post-menopausal. There is no more of the monthly bleeding, which indicates the body's ability to produce life. God, however, tells Abraham that Sarah *will* give birth at the corresponding time next year. Sarah laughed. It must have seemed so ridiculous to her—she was old and so was Abraham! Yet, this was the promise God left with them. It must have filled Sarah with enormous hope to know God would visit to *hand-deliver* a promise.

> Now Abraham journeyed from there toward the land of the Negev, and settled between Kadesh and Shur; then he sojourned in Gerar. Abraham said of Sarah his wife, "She is my sister." So Abimelech king of Gerar sent and took Sarah. (Genesis 20:1-2 NASB)

It makes perfect sense that once they were both filled with so much hope something would happen to threaten it. This time, Abraham and his family are journeying to an area between Kadesh and Shur (Genesis 20:1). The King of Gerar, Abimelech, notices Sarah because of her beauty—at 89 years old, wow! He takes her after Abraham (again) declares she is his sister. Not again! However, before Abimelech can touch her, God warns him in a dream to let her go. God made it clear that it was He who kept Abimelech from sinning against Him. There was still a promise on the table.

God had promised to make Abraham *a father of many nations*. He promised Kings would come forth from Sarah. I would imagine the years of waiting caused some weariness—even in the midst of their faithfulness. Sarah's journey had been tumultuous. She was taken as wife by a foreign king—not once, but twice. She concocted a disastrous idea to acquire a child—and her husband agreed to it. The maid she had hoped would help her was the first to betray her. In each instance, her husband's response is something less than we might expect of a lover and protector. Abraham made it clear that saying she was his sister would save *his* life. Then, he washed his hands of the whole Hagar mess.

In the midst of her faith-building journey God was with her. He was making provision for her and sustaining her. Sarah's has been a tough journey. Her road to destiny was a rocky one paved with barrenness, disappointment, betrayal and uncertainty. Yet after all of this, we find a beautiful insight about Sarah that Peter acknowledges in his first epistle. He highlights Sarah (who clearly had her own share of flaws) as a role model to other women when cultivating authentic beauty.

> For in this way in former times the holy women also, who hoped in God, used to adorn themselves, being submissive to their own husbands; just as Sarah obeyed Abraham, calling him lord, and you have become her children if you do what is right without being frightened by any fear. (1 Peter 3:5-6 NASB)

After everything that had happened, *Sarah obeyed Abraham, calling him Lord* . . . . Wow! You may be saying, "yeah . . . well that was Sarah . . . that was then, this is now—and I'm not her!" I am not able to tell you if Sarah was some huge spiritual giant. She is, however, noted in the hall of fame of faith in Hebrews 11. At this point, I offer you two clues as to the reasons Sarah is highlighted by God in this context and is worthy of our attention as well when it comes to *authentic beauty*. First, as noted in 1 Peter 3:5, *the basis of Sarah's faith was her hope in God*. It was not her hope in her husband's ability to hear from God. It was not hope in her husband's ability to make quality decisions or protect her from harm. It was her hope in God. In other words, her clothing was faith. Peter says it was how she adorned herself. *When faith is our adornment, we can survive the failure of people.* When faith is our adornment, we can overcome the poor choices of others. When faith is our outer garment, we can weather disappointment and trials at the hand of others.

> By faith even Sarah herself received ability to conceive, even beyond the proper time of life, since she considered Him faithful who had promised. (Hebrews 11:11 NASB)

Second, as Hebrews 11:11 points out, *Sarah believed that God was faithful.* He was faithful to keep His promises. Her faith in God was the catalyst for her body to receive the strength to accomplish something it was *physically* past being able to do. Though there was no evidence in her physical body she could give birth to a son, by faith she conceived and became the *mother of many nations.* I think these two points are very important when examining how offense can be avoided.

Sarah should have been able to rely upon her husband to protect and cover her especially in the episodes involving the foreign kings. Yet despite the disappointments and poor choices on Abram/Abraham's part, she was able to honor him as her husband, her shepherd and the love of her life. It's one of the reasons she is so special in Scripture. I can't imagine walking out what she endured. There's no hint of any lingering bitterness, resentment, or offense toward Abraham. Instead, God records that, *without fear,* she followed her husband. What a beautiful testimony God ascribes to her! *Sarah's hope was in God—in His character and His faithfulness.* Because her hope was in the right place, she could avoid the offense associated with being let down by someone she trusted.

Joseph . . . when betrayed by those closest to him

> When they saw him from a distance and before he came close to them, they plotted against him to put him to death.

They said to one another, "Here comes this dreamer! "Now then, come and let us kill him and throw him into one of the pits; and we will say, 'A wild beast devoured him.' Then let us see what will become of his dreams!" But Reuben heard *this* and rescued him out of their hands and said, "Let us not take his life." Reuben further said to them, "Shed no blood. Throw him into this pit that is in the wilderness, but do not lay hands on him"—that he might rescue him out of their hands, to restore him to his father. So it came about, when Joseph reached his brothers, that they stripped Joseph of his tunic, the varicolored tunic that was on him; and they took him and threw him into the pit. Now the pit was empty, without any water in it. Then they sat down to eat a meal. And as they raised their eyes and looked, behold, a caravan of Ishmaelites was coming from Gilead, with their camels bearing aromatic gum and balm and myrrh, on their way to bring *them* down to Egypt. Judah said to his brothers, "What profit is it for us to kill our brother and cover up his blood? "Come and let us sell him to the Ishmaelites and not lay our hands on him, for he is our brother, our *own* flesh." And his brothers listened *to him.* Then some Midianite traders passed by, so they pulled *him* up and lifted Joseph out of the pit, and sold him to the Ishmaelites for twenty *shekels* of silver. Thus they brought Joseph into Egypt. (Genesis 37:18-28 NASB)

When Joseph's brothers saw that their father was dead, they said, "What if Joseph bears a grudge against us and pays us back in full for all the wrong which we did to him!" So they sent *a message* to Joseph, saying, "Your father charged before he died, saying, 'Thus you shall say to Joseph, "Please forgive, I beg you, the transgression of your brothers and their sin, for they did you wrong." ' And now, please forgive the transgression of the servants of the God of your father."

And Joseph wept when they spoke to him. Then his brothers also came and fell down before him and said, "Behold, we are your servants." But Joseph said to them, "Do not be afraid, for am I in God's place? "As for you, you meant evil against me, *but* God meant it for good in order to bring about this present result, to preserve many people alive. "So therefore, do not be afraid; I will provide for you and your little ones." So he comforted them and spoke kindly to them. (Genesis 50:15-21 NASB)

Joseph's response to his situation is a tremendous demonstration of his emotional and spiritual maturity. Please indulge me for a moment. If there were ever a guy who might have had reason(s) to justify offense it was Joseph. Let's review some of the less pleasant moments of his life:

- His mother died when he was young.
- Though favored by his father, his older brothers hated him.
- At 17, he received a dream from the heart of God and was misunderstood by his family.
- His brothers, driven by jealousy and insecurity, devised a plan to kill him.
- He was betrayed and sold into slavery by his brothers.
- While conducting himself with honor and integrity as a slave, he was falsely accused of attempted rape.
- He graciously interpreted the dreams of fellow inmates, yet his benevolence was forgotten for two years (even after he begged them to remember him).
- He was separated from his father and family for 25 years because of the insecurity and selfishness of others.

On this side of history, we understand God was preparing and strategically positioning Joseph to deliver a small nation—a chosen people—from famine. He was also positioning and preparing that nation in order to grow them exponentially over the next 400 years. God had a plan. It was a plan that would not only save a nation, but it would also cut a path for the deliverance of people throughout eternity. Joseph, however, did not know God had a plan. Despite that, we never hear him grumble, carp, or whine. He walked out his trials with integrity, dignity and honor. Along the way, we read the commentary *the Lord was with him.* It doesn't mean, however, Joseph wasn't heartbroken or disappointed by the circumstances he encountered.

> He sent a man before them, Joseph, *who* was sold as a slave. They afflicted his feet with fetters, he himself was laid in irons; Until the time that his word came to pass, the word of the Lord tested him. (Psalm 105:17-19 NASB)

Each of the low points of Joseph's life was an opportunity to fall into the trap of offense. There were certainly people he could legitimately blame for his troubles. There were instigators and false accusers as well as those who were selfish and self-centered. Every ingredient Joseph would need to justify bad behavior was present, but he opted for a better choice. Despite what he encountered and the numerous trials he faced, he ultimately gave the world the correct opinion of His God. Joseph passed the test. In the end, Joseph was able to spiritually discern what was really taking place. God was on the move—strategically orchestrating a plan to ensure there was provision and safety for His covenant people.

So what can we take away from Joseph's response? It seems he understood the bigger picture. While it may be easier for many of us to see the bigger picture later in our lives, there is an indication of tremendous insight early in Joseph's life. When approached by Potiphar's wife, Joseph knew surrendering to her temptation was about more than the enjoyment of sin for a moment. It would be an affront to God. Joseph chose not to fall into the trap of offense. He chose not to blame, accuse, or harbor resentment. He made a conscious choice to honor God in his dealings with everyone he encountered. He was faithful in Potiphar's house though he didn't deserve to be there. He acted responsibly in the prison though punished under false accusation. He was benevolent to the baker and cupbearer in interpreting their dreams though he shouldn't even have been there with them. He opted to view his circumstances through God's eyes. Therefore, offense couldn't get a footing or a hold in Joseph's life.

Years later his brothers approached him after their father's death expecting to receive their comeuppance for their bad behavior. Joseph's spiritual acuity was sharp. He understood that the evil they intended for him was God's good hand moving in order to save the lives of many. Offense couldn't take root in his life because he maintained his focus on the Lord. He chose not to meditate on the bad behavior of others. Instead, he consciously processed how God had provided for and sustained him in a difficult season.

> Before the year of famine came, two sons were born to Joseph. Asenath, the daughter of Potiphera priest of On, bore them to him. Joseph called the name of the firstborn Manasseh. "For," he said, "God has made me forget all my hardship and all my father's house." The name of the second he called Ephraim, "For God has made me fruitful in the land of my affliction." (Genesis 41:50-52 ESV)

His sons' names reflect his understanding of God's sovereignty over his circumstances and God's provision in the midst of trial. Joseph's life reveals so much regarding our need to trust God with the larger plan of our lives.

David . . . when Nathan confronted him about Bathsheba

Then the LORD sent Nathan to David. And he came to him and said, "There were two men in one city, the one rich and the other poor. "The rich man had a great many flocks and herds. "But the poor man had nothing except one little ewe lamb which he bought and nourished; And it grew up together with him and his children. It would eat of his bread and drink of his cup and lie in his bosom, And was like a daughter to him. "Now a traveler came to the rich man, And he was unwilling to take from his own flock or his own herd, To prepare for the wayfarer who had come to him; Rather he took the poor man's ewe lamb and prepared it for the man who had come to him." *Then David's anger burned greatly against the man,* and he said to Nathan, "As the LORD lives, surely the man who has done this deserves to die. "He must make restitution for the lamb fourfold, *because he did this thing and had no compassion."* Nathan then said to David, " You are the man! Thus says the LORD God of Israel, ' It is I who anointed you king over Israel and it is I who delivered you from the hand of Saul. 'I also gave you your master's house and your master's wives into your care, and I gave you the house of Israel and Judah; and if that had been too little, I would have added to you many more things like these! 'Why have you despised the word of the LORD by doing evil in His sight? You have struck down Uriah the Hittite with the sword, have taken his wife to be your wife, and have killed him with the sword of the sons

of Ammon. 'Now therefore, the sword shall never depart
from your house, because you have despised Me and have
taken the wife of Uriah the Hittite to be your wife.' "Thus
says the Lord, 'Behold, I will raise up evil against you from
your own household; I will even take your wives before your
eyes and give *them* to your companion, and he will lie with
your wives in broad daylight. 'Indeed you did it secretly,
but I will do this thing before all Israel, and under the sun.'
" Then David said to Nathan, " I have sinned against the
LORD." And Nathan said to David, "The LORD also has
taken away your sin; you shall not die. (2 Samuel 12:1-13
NASB *emphasis mine*)

When Nathan confronted David, David confessed his sin and
repented. He didn't try to *manage the perception* Nathan had of him.
He didn't attempt to cover or excuse his sin once it had been exposed.
He also remained open to the remaining judgment that Nathan foretold
would befall him and his household.

Two significant factors may have contributed to the positive results
of Nathan's dialogue with David about his sin. The first and most
significant factor was David's heart. While Nathan's rebuke of David's
sin was packaged in a nonthreatening story it was no magic bullet.
No matter how beautifully Nathan may have packaged the story, true
repentance required a willing heart. David's own heart was the key
component for avoiding the snare of offense. David had to be willing
to receive the rebuke and *acknowledge his sin*. It was necessary in order
for repentance to take place. Once that happened, David acknowledged
and confessed his sin against God. God immediately forgave him and
removed his sin (2 Samuel 12:13). This is certainly worth remembering
in light of 1 John 1:9.

Second, Nathan used good judgment. He confronted David in a respectful way and avoided attacking David personally. He approached David with a story that was seemingly detached from who the king was. Nathan's approach to confronting David was a divinely inspired strategic move of God. The Lord guides him to speak in a way that taps into the true moral compass of David's heart. By approaching him with a story about someone else, it precluded David becoming defensive and rejecting the report of his own behavior. This is especially important since David was the King, and one word could have had Nathan executed. Nathan avoided accusing tones and personal attacks. Instead, he approached David with a very non-threatening story and provided a relevant example. Nathan framed it in a way that would allow David to understand the gravity of his sin and move toward repentance.

David first tapped into his own anger regarding the injustice of the situation (2 Samuel 12:5). Then, he locked in on the lack of compassion demonstrated by the rich man in Nathan's story (2 Samuel 12:6). Up to this point, David may have distanced himself from his sin. We know David knew he was wrong because he tried to hide his sin. Nathan successfully addressed the rebuke in a way David could hear it. Here, again, is a good lesson to model when it falls to us to lovingly correct or admonish a friend or loved one regarding their bad behavior.

Nathan's communication style was divinely inspired. While stories may sometimes come naturally, we're not always adept at the cross application of stories to our lives in helping us communicate more effectively. Nathan's motive was to communicate God's heart to a nation's leader. Incidentally, when we're called to correct or reprove others that should be our motive as well. David's response required an acknowledgement that what he was hearing wasn't about the prophet Nathan calling out a king's sin. It was about a loving heavenly Father who had been distanced by His son's disobedience. Reconciliation and redemption are important to God. He was trying to get David back to the place of drawing near to Him. God wanted David to acknowledge his sin and repent.

David . . . when assaulted by Shemei

> When King David came to Bahurim, behold, there came out from there a man of the family of the house of Saul whose name was Shimei, the son of Gera; he came out cursing continually as he came. He threw stones at David and at all the servants of King David; and all the people and all the mighty men were at his right hand and at his left. Thus Shimei said when he cursed, "Get out, get out, you man of bloodshed, and worthless fellow!" The LORD has returned upon you all the bloodshed of the house of Saul, in whose place you have reigned; and the LORD has given the kingdom into the hand of your son Absalom. And behold, you are taken in your own evil, for you are a man of bloodshed!" (2 Samuel 16:5-8 NASB)

Shemei was a relative of Saul's. He was angry and verbally accosting. Shemei had no problem hurling accusations, dust and stones at a King! He was irreverent, loud, indiscriminate and vicious. He also put out before everyone God's judgment regarding David. Despite all of that, David's response was to not be offended. He *chose* instead to view the whole episode as the providence of God. This must have been challenging for David. Even when the voices surrounding David were advocating that *he had the right to avenge himself* and that Shemei should be dealt with, David didn't take the bait. Instead he *entrusted himself to the righteous Judge.* He left room for God to oversee and handle the situation according to His own will.

David didn't try to manage the perceptions of Shemei or the servants and soldiers who were accompanying him. The truth is, the whole scene wore David and his company out physically and, perhaps, emotionally. Despite the toll it took on them, David never saw it as license to vindicate himself or those traveling with him. Here again is a great life lesson for us. David was in a position to *squash the noise* from Shemei. He was intentional, however, about leaving the details to God.

Again, the key component here was the state of David's heart. It was humble before the Lord. We also see David's submission to the absolute sovereignty of God (2 Samuel 16:10-11). Though he is king, he understands who truly rules and reigns. Consequently, David willingly humbled himself before the Lord.

Canaanite woman . . . when coming to Jesus for her daughter's healing

> Jesus went away from there, and withdrew into the district of Tyre and Sidon. And a Canaanite woman from that region came out and began to cry out, saying, "Have mercy on me, Lord, Son of David; my daughter is cruelly demon-possessed." But He did not answer her a word. And His disciples came and implored Him, saying, "Send her away, because she keeps shouting at us." But He answered and said, "I was sent only to the lost sheep of the house of Israel." But she came and began to bow down before Him, saying, "Lord, help me!" And He answered and said, "It is not good to take the children's bread and throw it to the dogs." But she said, "Yes, Lord; but even the dogs feed on the crumbs which fall from their masters' table." Then Jesus said to

her, "O woman, your faith is great; it shall be done for you as you wish." And her daughter was healed at once. (Matthew 15:21-28 NASB)

It would have been so easy in this circumstance to *walk away offended and wounded.* The woman could have allowed uncontrolled negative thoughts to send her down the wrong road. She could have been upset with the disciples for urging Jesus to send her away. She could have really taken issue with Jesus' comment about throwing food to dogs. In short, Jesus was saying to her, "I'm not here for you." She *chose*, however, to stay focused. Though there was the indication she was inadequate and didn't fit in, her focus stayed on the Christ who was in front of her—*who was more than adequate and who could never come up short.*

Her reply in verse 27 emphasizes two things—she wasn't interested in managing anyone's perception of her nor was she willing to argue about who she was or wasn't. More importantly, she understood who *He* was. Many might call her a dog, but she recognized the Master when she saw Him. No amount of formality or social rejection was going to keep her from the *deliverance* she wanted for her daughter. Her first response is, *"YES Lord . . . ."* What He was saying was true. Every defense was down—no smoke, no mirrors. *"Yes, it's true; I'm not worthy. I'm not one of you. The fact is I come from a base, idolatrous and irreverent culture."* She had no intention of arguing over her worthiness. In the end it boiled down to this: *"It doesn't matter who anyone thinks I am. What matters is I know who You are!"*

She avoided the snare of offense by continuing to maintain her focus on the one who was Master, Savior and King. By locking her sights on Him, she avoided being lured into the *pit of self-pity* and the *ditch of despair.* Her example offers us one of the most powerful models in Scripture. She moved past the naysayers, ignored the detractors, and dismissed condescending glances in order to pursue the Savior. What would our lives look like if we followed her example? What would our lives look like if we ignored those who call us names, marginalize us or dismiss our relevance? What would our lives look like if we continued to press in to know the Savior and experience Him no matter how difficult it sometimes seems?

Because she was Canaanite (and, thus, hated by the Jews in general), she probably brought her fair share of wounds with her. She didn't allow that to hinder her. She pressed on toward the Savior for what she knew He only could provide. She looked beyond being hated and socially ostracized. Her daughter needed deliverance and healing, and Jesus was the only Healer in town. This was no time to care about what others thought of her. The negative opinions of others couldn't add value to her situation, but the healing power of a living Savior could.

Now, notice Jesus didn't respond with, *"Oh, Canaanite woman, you've done such a great job not being offended—not being wounded."* No, He responded, "Your faith is great!" It means she was able to see past what she was experiencing in order to know God more intimately. Her faith propelled her past man's opinion and the trap of offense. So the question for us is: Do we have the faith to trust His character, His nature, His strength and His faithfulness despite what *others* may be thinking of us, saying about us, or doing to us?

John the Baptist . . . as his role neared fulfillment

And they came to John and said to him, "Rabbi, He who was with you beyond the Jordan, to whom you have testified, behold, He is baptizing and all are coming to Him." John answered and said, "A man can receive nothing unless it has been given him from heaven. "You yourselves are my witnesses that I said, 'I am not the Christ,' but, 'I have been sent ahead of Him." "He who has the bride is the bridegroom; but the friend of the bridegroom, who stands and hears him, rejoices greatly because of the bridegroom's voice. So this joy of mine has been made full. "He must increase, but I must decrease." (John 3:26-30 NASB)

John avoids offense by acknowledging that *he didn't own his calling* in the first place. It wasn't John who had elevated himself to the position of *one crying in the wilderness . . . to prepare the way of the Lord* (Mark 1:3). No, God handpicked him for *a specific purpose* and *window of time* in history. John knew the privilege he walked in was a tremendous gift from God. He understood that all of what he was experiencing was because of God's grace and by *sovereign* appointment. John viewed the transition as an opportunity to rejoice because the *Word of God was now flesh and was dwelling among them (John 1:14)*. He understood, though his role had been pivotal, it was now necessary for his influence to decrease. Messiah had come. It was now time for Christ to increase. Men would be drawn to Him. John clearly understood why he was on earth and the purposes for which he had been born.

John didn't allow the perceptions or discussions of others to influence or change the reality of his role in the kingdom. John's disciples were caught off guard and may have been intimidated by the fact that someone else in town was getting all of the baptism business. John wasn't undone by it at all. He embraced the privilege of the role he had in God's master plan. He knew very well who Jesus was. At the same time, he also knew (and this is important) who he was relative to Christ.

John wasn't trying to manage the perceptions of others. He understood his primary purpose in history was to point to the Messiah. He wouldn't let anyone twist or corrupt his purpose. This understanding kept John from being threatened by how AWESOME Jesus was (Matthew 11:6). In addition, it also set up a powerful leadership model for John's disciples in preparation for a transition that was just around the corner. In the end, God's testimony of John is that of those born of women, there is none greater (Matthew 11:11; Luke 7:28).

John's life also provides a beautiful glimpse into how we should respond when God moves us from obscurity to prominence. In our journey to beautiful, God will sometimes position us in unexpected roles. In those seasons, it's important to remember three things. First, *we've been sent or appointed by God.* We don't create the path to greatness or brilliance. Most of us are keenly aware that the path we would cut might look significantly different anyway. God has sent us. Our success in that role is directly tied to how we respond to His leading. Second, *remember whose mission it is.* It isn't our agenda or mission. It is His. He determines the degree of influence we have and the significance of our role. Lastly, *don't concern yourself with managing the perception of others.* There will always be a little voice (or a mob) chiding you to pay attention to the critics and the fans. Do yourself a favor—*ignore both and opt to respond only to the voice of God.*

4

Avoiding Offense
and Caring for Scars

At any given moment, each of us can find ourselves the casualty of offense. Some unexpected event may cause us to stumble or be snared by attitudes of pride, unforgiveness, resentment, anger, or bitterness. Our most effective strategies for dealing with those situations will have much to do with how prepared we are before we encounter them. We must be of sober spirit and on the alert to guard our hearts and minds.

> Therefore *humble yourselves* under the mighty hand of God, that He may exalt you at the proper time, casting all your anxiety on Him, because He cares for you. *Be of sober spirit, be on the alert.* Your adversary, the Devil, prowls around like a roaring lion, seeking someone to devour. But resist him, firm in your faith, knowing that the same experiences of suffering are being accomplished by your brethren who are in the world. After you have suffered for a little while, the God of all grace, who called you to His eternal glory in Christ, will Himself perfect, confirm, strengthen and establish you (1 Peter 5:6-10 NASB *emphasis mine*)

Entrust yourself to the righteous Judge. Jesus, of course, is our standard bearer in this area. Entrusting ourselves to the righteous Judge means we rest in the belief He knows better than we do what the future holds. He has plans that will benefit us. There will always be some attempt by the Devil to distort our perception, disrupt our lives and dash our hopes. Trusting God means believing He is fully aware of everything we are experiencing, and He is more than capable of helping us navigate every situation we face. It is about placing ourselves in His trust and care. It means believing that although our situation seems dire, it does not mean He has forgotten about us or has abandoned us.

Cultivate your love relationship with the Lord. Since the Enemy of our souls is always bombarding us with questions of inadequacy and inferiority, it is critical we press in to know how much God loves us. We cultivate a love relationship by spending time with Him. I love God's Word and understand the critical role it serves in my life. Remember, however, we aren't in a relationship with the book. We are in relationship with God through the Word who became flesh. Time in His Word is about cultivating our love for Him. The more we do this the more prone we are to see with His eyes, hear with His ears and feel with His heart. There is less chance of becoming ensnared if we are cultivating a deep love relationship with God. As our love for Him grows and thrives, we learn to desire the things that further our growth. We also learn to avoid patterns of behavior that disrupt our intimacy with Him.

Embrace the destiny God has for <u>YOU</u>. I'm amazed at how quickly we idolize, covet and mimic the patterns and successes of others. The business sector formalizes it by referring to it as *benchmarking*. We see successful or prosperous situations and assume that if it works for someone else, surely we must be entitled to the same successes as well. How willing are you to pursue and embrace God's desire for you personally—whatever it looks like? This requires a major paradigm shift for most of us. It means no matter what we see happening in the lives of others, we're not to compare it to what is happening in ours. It means yielding to the fulfillment of God's purposes and plans in our generation (Acts 13:36). It may mean setting aside our presumptuous personal agendas in order to make us available to God's agenda for our lives.

Recognize when offense is crouching at your door. Offense is looking for a home and wants to put down roots. Again, God's warning to Cain regarding his jealousy over his brother Abel's offering seems appropriate to address *offense* as well. God told Cain sin was crouching at the door and its desire was for him (Genesis 4:7). It was Cain who needed to master it in order to keep it from gaining power over him. We, too, need to understand that offense crouches at our door waiting to gain mastery over us. We won't *happen upon* a victory in this area. We need to be alert, intentional and strategic in this area. *Do not let offense in!* When fueled by our negative thought patterns, it's roots spread quickly.

Be willing to confess whatever sin is necessary to move forward. Remember that God is faithful and just to forgive us and cleanse us as we confess our sin (1 John 1:9). Come clean and be open about who and where you are. Be willing to respond with brokenness and humility when God lovingly calls you out. Believe that as you yield to His will, He will bring great change in your life. It is His desire to move in close to you. When we feel ourselves distanced from God, it usually isn't because He is the one who has withdrawn. It is because we have withdrawn ourselves from Him. *We distance ourselves by our disobedience or complacency.* This is what David understood as he penned the contents of Psalm 51. His own sin had separated him from God. When he acknowledged his sin, the Lord forgave him. He was able to return to intimate relationship with God the Father.

Acknowledge the reality of God's sovereignty in every situation. Whether we want to acknowledge it or not, He is sovereign. As I wrote earlier, this seems a big point in how Miriam erred. It was God Who gave Moses his authority. A clear understanding of that keeps us from stumbling over things that aren't our concern. Trust that God isn't caught off guard by your circumstances. He knew you'd be where you are before you got there, and He's been prepared *for a long time* to deal with you in that place. He understands very well the situation you're facing. He has a plan for you and will not give up on you.

Evicting unwelcome inhabitants

Remember healing is a process. Wounds need time to heal. Scars disappear over time, or . . . they don't. Whether they do or not, God has made you beautiful. Be diligent, however, to keep watch. Don't allow offense to creep in to establish residency.

> But if you do not drive out the inhabitants of the land from before you, then it shall come about that those whom you let remain of them will become as pricks in your eyes and as thorns in your sides, and they will trouble you in the land in which you live. (Numbers 33:55 NASB [cf. Exodus 23:20-33])

As He prepared them for the Promised Land, God warned Israel not to allow the inhabitants to *remain* in the land (Exodus 23:33). These other nations represented things that were foreign and contrary to the authentic spiritual nature of God's chosen people. The peoples, practices and influences of those nations would become a snare to them and eventually *vex* them. God warned the Hebrews there would be consequences if they did not drive out the unwelcome inhabitants.

Possessing the land meant removing those things that had no right to be there so they could freely inhabit and thrive in the land.

One way to avoid offense is to *take possession of your land* and *drive out unwelcome inhabitants*. Offense is an unwelcome inhabitant. If, however, you have invited offense into your life, it's time to evict it! When offense goes unresolved or sin goes unchecked it acquires the power to vex us. When we don't get rid of the things that hinder, they can gain a superiority or mastery over us (Genesis 4:7). When our wounds (from offenses, etc.) go unchecked or untreated, they disrupt and pollute our land. They hinder us from taking full possession of our inheritance. God's instructions to Israel were clear. If they allowed the inhabitants to remain, they would become pricks in their eyes, thorns in their sides and cause trouble. It is the same with offense. When we let it remain, it skews our vision, distorts our perspective and causes trouble.

In Numbers 33, we see God preparing His people to enter Promised Land. Their departure from Egypt represented a setting aside of old habits and behaviors that were no longer useful. During the 400 years they spent in Egypt, there would have been rituals and learned behaviors that may have become a part of their culture. Those patterns of behavior needed to be abandoned as God prepared to establish them as a nation. There may have also been cultural adaptations that needed to be stripped away in order to purify their identity with Yahweh. In many ways, it is the same for us. Offense and the associated bad behaviors are no longer useful for us. There are mindsets and thought processes that need to be abandoned and stripped away in order for us to possess our land the way we should.

Life in the Promised Land would have its own challenges. The inhabitants of the land would not be looking forward to Israel's arrival. The Israelites would have to be prepared as a people to encounter new challenges. There would be things they would need to guard against.

They would gradually learn and adapt to a new way of life in the Promised Land. Beloved, it will be the same for us. Learning to avoid offense means embracing the principles of God for victorious living. It means being willing to adopt new behaviors in order to avoid old traps and snares. It requires we be vigilant and always prepared to resist *unwelcome inhabitants* when they show up.

Possessing our land also means cleaning up what needs to be cleaned up. We will need to uproot the weeds of resentment, anger, bitterness, jealousy and apathy. We must make room for *quality plantings that produce beautiful fruit.* We will need to maintain the landscape—do whatever is necessary to ensure our land is not overrun or destroyed because of complacency and laziness. Kingdom living requires a new mindset that finds its grounding in the Word of God.

Caring for our scars

We've addressed how to avoid offense, but what do we do with the scars we bear from our wounds? We have made mistakes. For some of us our choices have been costly. We desperately need God to heal us and make our mess beautiful. Where do we begin? How about we start with the One who is intimately acquainted with everything we experience?

> So when it was evening on that day, the first day of the week, and when the doors were shut where the disciples were, for fear of the Jews, Jesus came and stood in their midst and said to them, "Peace be with you." And when He had said this, He *showed them both His hands and His side.* The disciples then rejoiced when they saw the Lord. So Jesus said to them again, "Peace be with you; as the Father has sent Me, I also send you." And when He had said this, He breathed on them and said to them, "Receive the Holy Spirit. "If you forgive

the sins of any, their sins have been forgiven them; if you retain the sins of any, they have been retained." But Thomas, one of the twelve, called Didymus, was not with them when Jesus came. So the other disciples were saying to him, "We have seen the Lord!" But he said to them, "Unless I see in His hands the imprint of the nails, and put my finger into the place of the nails, and put my hand into His side, I will not believe." After eight days His disciples were again inside, and Thomas with them. Jesus came, the doors having been shut, and stood in their midst and said, "Peace be with you." Then He said to Thomas, "Reach here with your finger, and see My hands; and reach here your hand and put it into My side; and do not be unbelieving, but believing." Thomas answered and said to Him, "My Lord and my God!" Jesus said to him, "Because you have seen Me, have you believed? Blessed are they who did not see, and yet believed." (John 20:19-29 NASB *emphasis mine*)

Jesus had scars after His resurrection. For Thomas, it would be the proof he would need as he encountered our resurrected Lord. Jesus began by showing them both His hands and His side. His scars were the testimony of God's faithfulness as well as the physical and visible proof that He was the Jesus they knew. Our scars can do the same for us. They reveal we've been through something. They may also serve as reminders of the greatness of God's grace and beautification as the One who brought us through our trials. It was Jesus who took the initiative to reveal and expose His scars. He didn't hide them; He also didn't shrink back as others looked at them. We sometimes view Thomas as a hardheaded skeptic because he refused to believe unless he saw the scars. However, his acknowledgement of Jesus as, "My Lord and My God" is also an acknowledgement of the power of God to restore, save and keep us eternally.

Jesus wasn't ashamed of His scars. Your scars may have left you feeling unworthy, unlovely and unbecoming emotionally and physically. They may represent the wounds of betrayal, rejection, or even your own hard-heartedness. At times, you may also feel compelled to vindicate yourself by offering explanations or placing blame as to why they exist. From your perspective, there is nothing lovely or beautiful about them. However, when you can look at the scar (the failure, disappointment and mistake) and rejoice in God's faithfulness because of what He's brought you through, another level of victory can be achieved. When Jesus showed the disciples His scars, they rejoiced to see *Him*. Yes, he had scars. More importantly, though, He *was present with them and in their midst.* They were able to touch, feel and experience Him—God had kept His promise.

Some might argue that Jesus having scars isn't a fair example because . . . well, He IS Jesus! It's important to remember Jesus set aside His deity when He was born in the flesh. On the cross, His Father rejected him because He took on our sin. Scripture makes it clear God made Him who knew no sin to be sin for us (2 Corinthians 5:21). He completely understands the shame and guilt associated with our emotional wounds and scars. In fact, He understands it better than anyone we know. This makes His willingness to share His scars even more significant because *His scars didn't showcase His sin; they revealed the penalty for our sin!*

He bore every bit of the weight of punishment for our sin. He experienced the pain of the death God owed to you and me because of our sin. He openly yielded Himself to a humiliating and brutal death just so He could reveal the scars in His hands, feet and sides. His willingness to reveal His scars is a reminder of the victory He obtained in rising from the dead. He conquered death and the grave. We don't have to live in the grip of shame and guilt. We're free and have risen to new life in Christ.

Perhaps you often reflect on the scar and still feel devastated by the hurt, loss, or pain. You find yourself sucked back into a place of offense, anger, bitterness, or something worse. It may be an indication there are still layers with which you need to deal. Don't panic—He who began a good work in you will be faithful to complete His work (Philippians 1:6). In fact, if our scars evoke that response from us it may be a good thing. It means our scars are doing their job. Part of the scar's job is to *shore up* our testimony. They serve as signposts to alert us to possible *areas of instability and tenderness.* They are opportunities for change and transformation.

PART 2

He Makes All things Beautiful By Invading Our World

*I*nvading our world is a reference to the experience of God's presence and intervention in our lives. This intervention can occur in various ways. There is the day-to-day intervention that happens around us all of the time though we often overlook it.

> It is because of Your mercy that we are not consumed. Your compassion never fails us; they are new every morning and great is Thy faithfulness. (Lamentations 3:22 NASB)

God's mercy and grace are newly available to us every morning. Every new sunrise we experience is confirmation that a new day of grace and mercy are available for us to draw upon. The really great news is He's faithful to maintain His commitment. *The availability of this mercy and grace are based solely on His character not ours.* He's at work all around us every day causing everything to work together for our good (Romans 8:28). He won't forget about or abandon us. Even when it appears He's not on the scene, He is intimately acquainted with every detail of our existence. With the same exacting detail to attention

He demonstrated at Creation *in the beginning,* He is attending to every detail of our lives. He sees us, He understands us and He loves us. He is for us, on our side and ordering our steps. There are no, "I shoulda had a V8," moments in the throne room. He knows our frame and our frailty (Psalm 103:14). He's intentional regarding His design and plan for our lives. He is ours, and we are His Beloved. He dwells within us by His Spirit, and He has called us His own.

The second way He intervenes reveals some of the more dramatic ways He moves in our lives. We know He is there facilitating our growth and moving on our behalf, but we may not be able to connect all of the dots. It's these moments I want to point out in this section. They are names you will recognize and stories with which you're familiar. They are *beautiful* illustrations of God's readiness to draw near to us and of His willingness to continue to create within us and around us for His glory.

5

God's Invasion of Their World

Rahab

Then Joshua the son of Nun sent two men as spies secretly from Shittim, saying, "Go, view the land, especially Jericho." So they went and came into the house of a harlot whose name was Rahab, and lodged there. (Joshua 2:1 NASB)

Now before they lay down, she came up to them on the roof, and said to the men, "I know that the Lord has given you the land, and that the terror of you has fallen on us, and that all the inhabitants of the land have melted away before you. "*For we have heard* how the Lord dried up the water of the Red Sea before you when you came out of Egypt, and what you did to the two kings of the Amorites who were beyond the Jordan, to Sihon and Og, whom you utterly destroyed. "*When we heard it,* our hearts melted and no courage remained in any man any longer because of you; for the Lord your God, *He is God in heaven above and on earth beneath.* "Now therefore, please swear to me by the Lord, since I have dealt kindly with you, that you also will deal kindly with my father's household, and give me a pledge of truth, and spare my father and my mother and my brothers and my sisters, with all who belong to them, and deliver our lives from death." So the men said to her, "Our life for yours if you do not tell this business of ours; and it shall come about when the Lord gives us the land that we will deal kindly and faithfully with you." (Joshua 2:8-14 NASB *emphasis mine*)

Her World

As the spies enter the city of Jericho, we are introduced to Rahab, the harlot. She lived in a walled city in fear of the God of the Hebrews. She lived with a daily awareness of His power and might as stories of the Hebrew God and His people circulated throughout the region. She had heard reports of the Hebrew God. When she met the spies, she was prepared to welcome, hide and help them. Despite the fact that the presence of the Israelites created fear within the nations around them, Rahab understood the power and the glory regarding the Hebrew God. She had heard and believed. Though the city of Jericho and the surrounding nations were experiencing fear, her faith both fueled and facilitated a vision for her own future.

God's Invasion

We don't how or why she became a prostitute. We're not familiar with her history and experiences. We're not privy to her emotional wounds or the scars she bore. Though history may always characterize her as a prostitute, it must also acknowledge her as a part of the scarlet thread of redemption[16] woven into the life of every believer in Christ. The first thing we see is her faith, which played out in how she helped the spies. She hid them and sent the search party on a wild goose chase. She knew that in order to be *saved*, she needed to connect herself to

God through His people. She struck a bargain with the spies that if she hid them, didn't warn of their attack and tied the scarlet thread in the window she and everyone with her would be protected, delivered and saved. I can just imagine the dialogue that may have occurred with her family members:

Family: "I hear soldiers . . . ."

Rahab: "I know . . . don't worry."

Family: "But they're killing everyone and destroying the city."

Rahab: "Don't panic, they promised they would spare/save us."

Family: "Four of our neighbors' homes are on fire . . . . ."

Rahab: "It's okay! Everything may fall apart around us, but the spies said they would come to rescue us."

Family: "But . . . but . . . but."

Rahab: "Listen, there is a scarlet thread hanging in that window; the spies promised me that if I helped them and hung the scarlet thread that I would not be destroyed. They also said my family would be spared. I trust they'll keep their word."

To fully appreciate the significance of the scarlet thread and God's plan of redemption in Rahab's story, we must rewind about 40 years to Israel's exodus from Egypt.

> And you shall not leave any of it over until morning, but whatever is left of it until morning, you shall burn with fire. 'Now you shall eat it in this manner: {with} your loins girded, your sandals on your feet, and your staff in your hand; and you shall eat it in haste—it is the LORD'S Passover. 'For I will go through the land of Egypt on that night, and will strike down all the firstborn in the land of Egypt, both man and beast; and against all the gods of Egypt I will execute

judgments—I am the LORD.' The blood shall be a sign for you on the houses where you live; and when I see the blood I will pass over you, and no plague will befall you to destroy you when I strike the land of Egypt. (Exodus 12:10-13 NASB)

In Exodus 12, Moses instructed the Hebrews to kill a lamb and, using hyssop, paint blood on the doorpost of their homes. The blood would indicate to the destroyer angel that the house was to be passed over—*death and destruction would pass over those who inhabited the home.* The event was also a *type* to show us what our salvation would look like in Christ—*His blood applied to our lives results in God's wrath passing over us.* His blood atones for our sin and cleanses us of unrighteousness.

Rahab's scarlet thread is representative of the *blood on the doorpost* during the Passover. The scarlet thread meant destruction would *passover* her home and family. Rahab and her family would experience their own Passover as the death and destruction intended for Jericho avoided coming near them. The scarlet thread would also be an indication of God's willingness to *graft in* those who were outsiders and outliers (Romans 11:11-24). It provided a glimpse of how God would bring to pass His promise to make Abraham the father of many nations. This prostitute, harlot, and outlier was positioned to be saved and would play a significant role in Jewish history and in the lineage of Christ. Despite what was going on around her, she held on to her testimony.

Joshua said to the two men who had spied out the land, " Go into the harlot's house and bring the woman and all she has out of there, as you have sworn to her." So the young men who were spies went in and brought out Rahab and her father and her mother and her brothers and all she had; they also brought out all her relatives and placed them outside the camp of Israel. They burned the city with fire, and all that was in it. Only the silver and gold, and articles of bronze and iron, they put into the treasury of the house of the LORD. However, Rahab the harlot and her father's household and all she had, Joshua spared; and she has lived in the midst of Israel to this day, for she hid the messengers whom Joshua sent to spy out Jericho. (Joshua 6:22-25 NASB)

After delivering her family, they set them outside the camp. Rahab lived in the midst of Israel. She built relationships, had a family, put down roots and established a presence. She lived *in the midst* of Israel—not on the periphery and not on the outside. At some point, she moved past the *harlot—prostitute—Jericho* stigma and moved forward to living in the midst of a people, embracing a new identity and being positioned to be part of a legacy that impacts eternity. Read that last sentence again . . . . We are called to the same task. At some point, we must move past our history, failures and wounds. We must move forward to embrace our identity in Christ and allow Him to establish a legacy through us as well.

Later in Scripture, we will know Rahab as King David's great, great, grandmother. When the story of the Messiah's birth is recounted, her name will be mentioned (Matthew 1:5). However, at that point, she's no longer Rahab, the harlot. She is Rahab, wife of Salmon, mother of Boaz. We know her name because of God's commitment to keep His promise. Hebrews 11:31 begins with the words, *"By faith Rahab . . . ."* In the midst of turbulent times, Rahab's faith in God was the basis of her salvation.

God invaded her world and made it beautiful. He took a woman's ugly situation and history, and He transformed it into something that would impact all of mankind for eternity. Everything about her was socially unacceptable and inadequate. However, in God's hands she was transformed into something beautiful. He established through her a legacy that is available to anyone who feels wounded, cast aside, marginalized, or dismissed.

The Shunammite Woman

One day Elisha went on to Shunem, where a wealthy woman lived, who urged him to eat some food. So whenever he passed that way, he would turn in there to eat food. And she said to her husband, "Behold now, I know that this is a holy man of God who is continually passing our way. Let us make a small room on the roof with walls and put there for him a bed, a table, a chair, and a lamp, so that whenever he comes to us, he can go in there." (2 Kings 4:8-10 ESV)

And he said, "What then is to be done for her?" Gehazi answered, "Well, she has no son, and her husband is old." He said, "Call her." And when he had called her, she stood in the doorway. And he said, "At this season, about this time next year, you shall embrace a son." And she said, "No, my lord, O man of God; do not lie to your servant." But the woman conceived, and she bore a son about that time the following spring, as Elisha had said to her. When the child had grown, he went out one day to his father among the reapers. And he said to his father, "Oh, my head, my head!" The father said to his servant, "Carry him to his mother." And when he had lifted him and brought him to his mother, the child sat on her lap till noon, and then he died. And she went up and laid him on the bed of the man of God and shut the door behind him and went out. (2 Kings 4:14-21 ESV)

Her World

She was prominent and benevolent. She prepared a spare room for the prophet Elisha and his servant Gehazi. Though she was married, her husband was old. She was also perceptive and spiritually discerning.

She was willing to make room for the Prophet who passed through regularly. She appeared to possess all she needed and was pleased with her life. She also didn't seem to desire accolades or recognition; she was content with the life she lived. However, somewhere deep within her there was a longing. It was a longing she may have placed on the back burner of her life. She pushed it away from the forefront of her mind—perhaps because of her husband's age. Her response to Elisha in 2 Kings 4:16, indicates the impact his prophecy had on her. It was *too wonderful* to believe it could happen, and she would be devastated if it were a cruel hoax.

God's Invasion

Just as Elisha had prophesied, the Shunammite conceived and gave birth to a son. What a glorious experience it must have been for her to hold her child after seasons of waiting! As she opened her heart and her home to make room for the Prophet Elisha, God opened her womb and made room for a son. We don't know much about the child's life except that he grew old enough to help his father in the fields reaping the harvest. At some point on a particular day, the child complained of a headache and was sent back to his mother where he eventually died in her arms. Without skipping a beat, she laid the child on the bed in the room she had prepared for the Prophet. She then traveled to find Elisha. I can't imagine the thoughts that may have raced through her mind as she made the journey. She told the driver not to slow down during the trip unless she said so. Elisha saw her coming from far off, yet God had hidden from his heart the serious nature of her visit. Her response to his greeting is simple, "All is well." (2 Kings 4:26 ESV)

She hadn't asked God for son, and she never wanted to be hurt. From her perspective, she was content with her lot in life. Why would

God grant such a tremendous blessing only to take it away? God's invasion of her world wasn't just about her or her son. It was about manifestations of God's glory. It was about His willingness and ability to make provision for His people.

> Then he summoned Gehazi and said, "Call this Shunammite." So he called her. And when she came to him, he said, "Pick up your son." She came and fell at his feet, bowing to the ground. Then she picked up her son and went out. (2 Kings 4:36-37 ESV)

Elisha traveled back to her home and raised her son from the dead (2 Kings 4:27-37). Elisha would later give her advance warning of a seven-year famine that would ravage the land (2 Kings 8:1-6). He instructed her to dwell in the land of the Philistines during that period of time. This would be God's provision for her and her family during difficult times. Following the famine, God would further provide for her by bringing her to the attention of the King who would also restore all of her land and all of the produce of her fields from the time the famine began.

By that time, her son was seven years older. Even he must have been aware of the testimony of his life and the role the prophet Elisha had played in it. The end result of God's invasion of the Shunammite's world is that *she had a testimony.* God invaded her world when the Prophet showed up traveling through town. It was a journey he made on a regular basis. Perhaps, it was God's intention all along to give her a child. Maybe He wanted to see if she would open the doors of her home as well as the door of her heart. *He was waiting for her to make room for Him.* Her perception of the holy man is the first indication of her openness. She accurately perceives the sanctity of the moment and responds with an open heart.

Hannah

> Now this man used to go up year by year from his city to worship and to sacrifice to the Lord of hosts at Shiloh, where the two sons of Eli, Hophni and Phinehas, were priests of the Lord. On the day when Elkanah sacrificed, he would give portions to Peninnah his wife and to all her sons and daughters. *But to Hannah he gave a double portion, because he loved her, though the Lord had closed her womb.* And her rival used to provoke her grievously to irritate her, because the Lord had closed her womb. So it went on year by year. As often as she went up to the house of the Lord, she used to provoke her. Therefore Hannah wept and would not eat. And Elkanah, her husband, said to her, "Hannah, why do you weep? And why do you not eat? And why is your heart sad? Am I not more to you than ten sons?" (1 Samuel 1:3-8 NASB *emphasis mine*)

Her World

Hannah was one of two wives. While that wasn't uncommon during those times, she was also childless. The second wife, Peninah, apparently had more than a few children. Elkanah, however, dearly loved Hannah. Though it is clear he treasured and valued her, she still longed for a child. Peninah continually tormented her. It would have been challenging to live in that culture and not have children. To also be tormented by a rival wife may have made it unbearable. From year to year, the family would travel to Shiloh for annual worship. Elkanah would pack up his wives, children and servants and make the annual trek to spend time in the presence of God. Each year, Hannah had to put up with Peninah's teasing and chiding her about being barren and childless. Hers was a situation awaiting God's invasion.

God's Invasion

God's invasion of Hannah's world was about much more than dealing with the oppression and affliction of her barrenness. Hannah's barrenness would provoke something specific from her. It would cause her to pray and cry out to God in a particular way. Her prayer would be the catalyst for a series of events that would move God's people in the direction He intended for them. If we look at her situation narrowly, it appears to be about a barren woman who longed to have a child. However, if we widen our purview, we see how even a character like Peninah plays a vital role in our sanctification before the Lord.

Peninah's tormenting coupled with God's closing of Hannah's womb created a temporal situation that may have been unbearable for Hannah. Though it seems Elkanah adored her, her heart's desire was still to have a child—to be a mother. Year after year, she made the journey to Shiloh and endured Peninah's torment. That convergence of circumstances facilitated the emotional and spiritual climate necessary to move Hannah to pour her heart out before the Lord in the Temple and before the Priest Eli.

As she prayed, she acknowledged her own affliction and the pain she had endured. The most profound aspect of her prayer, however, was her declaration and commitment to return to the Lord the very child she was asking of Him *before she ever received the child from the Lord.* Her prayer reveals something about her heart. She understood that though she would conceive and give birth to a son, the child would belong to the Lord. The baby was the Lord's treasure, and she would share the privilege of shepherding over the child's soul for a season. Her commitment to *give him to the Lord* is her acknowledgement of God's sovereignty over every aspect of her life. It is also a beautiful picture of *receiving from the Lord with open hands and leaving them open in God's presence.* On the heels of her petition, God moved on her behalf.

God remembered Hannah—He took notice of her. His next move wasn't simply about Hannah; it was also about His covenant people. The Lord remembered her, and she gave birth to a son, Samuel. She acknowledged in naming him that he was the answer to her prayers (1 Samuel 1:20). After he was weaned, Hannah made the trip to Shiloh *again to worship*. This time, Peninah wouldn't be able to torment her. Even if she did, it wouldn't matter. With the help of the Lord, Hannah had weathered the trial of barrenness. She had survived the fiery darts of accusation, ridicule and torment. She had overcome Peninah's chiding and meanness. She had walked with God through the valley of emptiness and remorse, and God's sovereignty had prevailed.

She had a child from the Lord. Hannah knows God—she has seen Him move on her behalf. She was holding the truth of His Word, His faithfulness and His grace in her hands as she made the trip to worship. When she arrived, from the same open hands with which she received Samuel, she presented him to the Lord to serve Him forever. So, Hannah dedicated Samuel to the Lord and worshipped the Lord at Shiloh.

Hannah's prayer in 1 Samuel 2:1-10 is very different from the prayer years before. The Lord had filled her cup. She is thriving in His presence. Hannah knows there is no one like the Lord—He is her Rock and Salvation. Before Samuel's birth, we saw a frail, afflicted and victimized woman. Now we see strength, dignity and courage. She had found her *strength* in the Lord. She maintained her *dignity* and honor as she waited on the Lord to answer her prayer. She found the *courage* to keep the commitment she made before the Lord and to dedicate her son to serve Him forever. With an open hand, she returned what she had received. The Lord blessed her again, and she went on to have three more sons and two daughters.

God had invaded Hannah's world. Samuel's birth wasn't only about Hannah. It was about what God wanted to do in the lives of His people. Hannah became a conduit for God's blessings on the children of Israel by raising a Prophet who had a heart for God. Samuel would go on to glorify the Lord with his life and his service in the Kingdom of God.

Zechariah and Elizabeth

> In the days of Herod, king of Judea, there was a priest named Zechariah, of the division of Abijah. And he had a wife from the daughters of Aaron, and her name was Elizabeth. And they were both righteous before God, walking blamelessly in all the commandments and statutes of the Lord. But they had no child, because Elizabeth was barren, and both were advanced in years. (Luke 1:5-7 ESV)

> And there appeared to him an angel of the Lord standing on the right side of the altar of incense. And Zechariah was troubled when he saw him, and fear fell upon him. But the angel said to him, "Do not be afraid, Zechariah, for your prayer has been heard, and your wife Elizabeth will bear you a son, and you shall call his name John. And you will have joy and gladness, and many will rejoice at his birth, for he will be great before the Lord. And he must not drink wine or strong drink, and he will be filled with the Holy Spirit, even from his mother's womb. And he will turn many of the children of Israel to the Lord their God, and he will go before him in the spirit and power of Elijah, to turn the hearts of the fathers to the children, and the disobedient to

the wisdom of the just, to make ready for the Lord a people prepared." (Luke 1:11-17 ESV)

Their World

They lived during the days of Herod. Zechariah was a priest who served in the Temple. Elizabeth was a daughter of Aaron. They lived on the cusp of God breaking His 400-year silence. He was now strategically positioning key people who would usher in the coming of the Messiah. Zechariah and Elizabeth were people who were righteous and walked blamelessly regarding the Commandments of the Lord.

All seemed well with them. However, they were an older couple, Elizabeth was barren and they had no children. They had been praying for years for a child despite Elizabeth's barrenness. Though their prayers appeared to be unanswered, they continued to serve the Lord and lived righteously before Him. Although the desire of their hearts had not been granted, they did not abandon their love for God or service in His presence.

God's Invasion

Zechariah was completing his rotation for duties in the Temple. He was in the midst of his daily life when God invaded his world in a profound way. The angel Gabriel appeared to him to let him know their prayers had been heard. Elizabeth would give birth to a son who would be filled with the Holy Spirit while still in his mother's womb. Their son would turn the hearts of many back to the Lord.

God invaded Zechariah and Elizabeth's world during the course of their daily lives. In the midst of circumstances that were less than ideal, God arrived to bring news of a blessing that would not only encourage these parents but also spark a chain of events to *make ready a people prepared for the Lord* (Luke 1:17). They were a couple advanced in years. They had faithfully served the Lord. From what we can tell, they may have been content to do so all the days of their lives. So, how does God make their situation beautiful? *He strengthens their faith.*

Though Zechariah served faithfully as a priest, there may have been a loss of hope in some area of his life. Even among those who love God, there can be seasons where we grow weary or our hope grows fragile. Our service to the Lord can become rote. We do what we know to do—what we feel we are supposed to do—void of any real motivation, hope, or faith. Zechariah had been praying for a child, but maybe he wasn't sure if God would answer. Gabriel exposes his unbelief. That had to be quite a shocker for a Temple priest. God would use this situation to ignite renewed faith in Zechariah and advance the Kingdom of God.

Elizabeth was also encouraged. God had looked on her with favor and removed her disgrace (Luke 1:25). Elizabeth had received the desire of her heart. Six months after conceiving, her cousin Mary visited her. The child in Elizabeth's womb leaped at the sound of Mary's voice (Luke 1:39-45). God had again sent confirmation that His power and anointing were present in their situation *and* on the child in Elizabeth's womb. Even as she awaited the birth of her child, she may have found it an interesting experience that Zechariah was unable to speak during her pregnancy.

It is evident that God's blessing on Zechariah and Elizabeth was not simply about them as a couple or the child who would be born. It was about what God wanted to do in the community of faith. It was about His blessings and how those blessings would influence those around them. The birth of John, the removal of Elizabeth's shame and the return of Zechariah's speech would all serve as testimonies of

God's greatness. The events would point to God's dynamic and active presence in their lives. Their situation would showcase His intentionality regarding even the smallest details of our lives. John's ministry, too, would go on to have an eternal impact. In fact, Christ said of him that of those born of women there is none greater (Matthew 11:11).

The Woman at the well

> A woman from Samaria came to draw water. Jesus said to her, "Give me a drink." (For his disciples had gone away into the city to buy food.) The Samaritan woman said to him, "How is it that you, a Jew, ask for a drink from me, a woman of Samaria?" (For Jews have no dealings with Samaritans.) Jesus answered her, "If you knew the gift of God, and who it is that is saying to you, 'Give me a drink,' you would have asked him, and he would have given you living water. (John 4:7-10 ESV)

Her World

She was a Samaritan—a natural enemy of the Jews. She had been married five times and was presently living with another man who wasn't her husband. Five marriages indicated, at least, five instances of broken covenant as well as five episodes of rejection, betrayal and abandonment. The fact that she was now living with another man was an indication there was an emptiness that needed to be filled in her life. She was wounded, hardened and embittered by failed marriages and social derision.

God's Invasion

As this woman goes to collect water at Jacob's well, she encountered her Deliverer. God's invasion of her world is beautiful. In the midst of her wounds, bitterness, hurt and sin Jesus makes *living water* available to her. *The Lord begins His invasion into her world by inviting her into His.* She is, at first, disarmed by His request for water. Instead of giving Him water and helping to quench the thirst of the Stranger, she rebukes Him for asking because of the known tensions between the Jews and the Samaritans. When presented with an opportunity to be a blessing, she chose instead to inflict a jab. Maybe it was because of the years of scorn the Samaritans suffered at the hand of the Jews, or, perhaps it was because as someone who was wounded herself, she was prone to wound others.

Instead of responding to her *redirect*, Jesus focused on the core issue at hand, *"If you knew the gift of God, and who it is . . . ."* It hits directly to the point: *she thought He was like everyone else*—like all of the other Jews. Maybe she even thought He was like all other men, but this was no ordinary Jew and, certainly, no ordinary man. He was *the one man* who could love her like none of her previous husbands could have loved her. He was *the one man* who could provide a love that would minister to and heal her deepest wounds. He was *the one man* who could provide living water that would satisfy her forever.

She made the same mistake many of us make when God invades our world. We focus so much on our own inadequacies and the shortcomings of others that *we underestimate God's ability to transform our lives by His very presence in it.* We contemplate all of the reasons why He shouldn't care about us. We rehearse over and over again our failures and how they impact our lives and the lives of those around us. Sometimes the Father will say to us *"Do, go, give . . . ."* Instead of just responding to

His promptings, we question *why* He wants us to "Do, go, give . . . ." We remind ourselves of all the reasons why we are the last person He should want to help or love. As a result, I think we miss many of our opportunities to embrace all the Savior wants to be in our lives. We forget we are His masterpiece, and He is at work continually making us more magnificent everyday. We also forget that His work in us is not only about us, but also about His glory—communicating to the world His nature and character through His interaction in our lives.

We see the Savior meet her right where she is. She had no idea this encounter would change her life forever. Her focus was on her past hurt and her present need. His focus was on healing her hurt, bringing true satisfaction to fill her present need, and establishing a secure future for her.

He then tells her to go get her husband. I have always wondered why He told her to get him. Was it to gain credibility with her so she would understand He wasn't just any guy sitting on the side of a well? Perhaps, it was to see how truthful and transparent she would be with Him. Her willingness to say she had no husband may have revealed an area of vulnerability. That vulnerability became *His door to her heart*. With His entry into her heart, her life and the lives of many in her city were transformed into something beautiful.

The man born blind

> As He passed by, He saw a man blind from birth. And His disciples asked Him, "Rabbi, who sinned, this man or his parents, that he would be born blind?" Jesus answered, "*It was* neither *that* this man sinned, nor his parents; but *it was* so that the works of God might be displayed in him. "We must work the works of Him who sent Me as long as it is day; night is coming when no one can work. "While I am in

the world, I am the Light of the world." When He had said this, He spat on the ground, and made clay of the spittle, and applied the clay to his eyes, and said to him, "Go, wash in the pool of Siloam" (which is translated, Sent). So he went away and washed, and came *back* seeing. (John 9:1-7 NASB)

His World

He was blind from birth—he had never been able to see. He relied on others for provision and protection. His vision was limited to only what he could imagine. He did not even know what it meant to see. He had never seen his parents' faces, a sunrise, or a sunset. Frankly, he had no idea of what he might be missing. As Jesus is passing by with them, the disciples ask, *"Who sinned . . . ."* Really? I thought about this for a while when I read it a few times. What a horrible question to ask! There are a lot of questions you might ponder when passing a blind man. I'm not sure that's a good question. However as I thought more about it I realized I might ask the same question. My question, however, might come from a darker place than the disciples' question. My question might flow from a *self-righteous, judgmental, and critical attitude.*

Consider for a moment how you might feel if you had a physical disability (or some unpleasant life situation) and, every time you were out in public, people began wondering who in your family sinned. Imagine how it might affect you if people looked at you and wondered *what your daddy did* to cause your dilemma! It would be devastating to most of us to live out that sort of existence—to know that others were always thinking the worst of us. Yet that is the question the disciples asked.

He had been condemned and rejected from birth because of his disabilities. There may have always been someone in a corner or on the sidelines speculating about his behavior, his parents' behavior, or his ancestry. He may not have known who spoke the words, but he still may have heard them. His parents and family members may also have been judged and rejected as neighbors and friends questioned what sin was responsible for his trials.

God's Invasion

The man is minding his own business when God reaches into his obscurity and brings him center stage. Not only is his affliction brought to the forefront, but the question of whose sin was responsible was also brought to the forefront. His lifetime affliction will now command a different type of attention. With a single act, God will transform his life and the lives of those around him. God will shift the paradigm regarding trials, suffering and physical affliction. Trials and suffering will no longer be viewed as indicators for *what someone has done wrong*. These same trials would now be opportunities for God's glory and power to be manifested among His people. His divine activity in their situations will showcase His righteousness and majesty. He will expand the purview of His disciples regarding Kingdom dynamics and God's sovereignty.

Jesus began by healing the blind man on the Sabbath. It was God's intention to invade this man's world on the Sabbath as a testimony to His own sovereignty, lordship and might. We know from Scripture Jesus only did what He saw the Father do. God was creating an opportunity for new vision—not only in the blind man's life but also in the lives of those around him. He had lived with disability, rejection and ridicule. Remember, even the disciples asked, *"Who did sin . . . ?"* The natural assumption was that someone must have done something wrong. If no one had done anything wrong, why was he not born whole—complete? God used this opportunity to open the blind eyes of those around the man as well.

Jesus' response highlights two important factors. First, with His response that *no one had sinned*. He vindicates the blind man and his parents. Since birth, he and his parents may have been judged and ostracized as people wondered about their holiness. Jesus makes it clear there is no sin that is being punished—this was done for God's glory. It may be difficult to contemplate that God would allow a man to go through his whole life blind in order to bring Himself glory. We might ask, *"Wouldn't You get more glory if he had been healed at birth or as a child?"* What I eventually come back to is God's declaration in Romans 8:28.

> And we know that for those who love God all things work together for good, for those who are called according to his purpose. (Romans 8:28 ESV)

This truth points to the second important factor that can be highlighted from the blind man's story. As Jesus healed the man, more than one set of blind eyes was opened that day. The blind man was healed of a lifelong affliction. Everyone who stood and watched had his or her eyes opened as well. They saw Jesus—Healer, Deliverer, Friend and Messiah. They observed God's mercy, grace and compassion at work. They saw a life transformed by the touch of the Master. They watched as guilt and shame were lifted. They saw healing take place. They saw God transform one family's situation into something beautiful. *Many eyes were opened that day as God invaded a blind man's world.*

It was God's intention to give vision to those in the city that day. When John chapter 9 begins, we see a man blind from birth—a beggar. By verse 30, the same man (who is no longer blind) is preaching to the

Pharisees about the credibility of Jesus' ministry. As the chapter ends, he declares that Jesus is Lord. For those who insisted they already knew the truth, God was exposing their blindness, arrogance, ignorance and sinfulness. For those who believed that day, God granted new vision.

The Man at Bethesda Pool

> After these things there was a feast of the Jews, and Jesus went up to Jerusalem. Now there is in Jerusalem by the sheep *gate* a pool, which is called in Hebrew Bethesda, having five porticoes. In these lay a multitude of those who were sick, blind, lame, and withered, [waiting for the moving of the waters; for an angel of the Lord went down at certain seasons into the pool and stirred up the water; whoever then first, after the stirring up of the water, stepped in was made well from whatever disease with which he was afflicted.] A man was there who had been ill for thirty-eight years. When Jesus saw him lying *there*, and knew that he had already been a long time *in that condition,* He said to him, "Do you wish to get well?" The sick man answered Him, "Sir, I have no man to put me into the pool when the water is stirred up, but while I am coming, another steps down before me." Jesus said to him, "Get up, pick up your pallet and walk." Immediately the man became well, and picked up his pallet and *began* to walk. Now it was the Sabbath on that day. (John 5:1-9 NASB)

His World

An angel would visit the pool at certain seasons to stir the waters. This stirring brought with it healing and deliverance. Whoever made it into the pool first, would be healed from whatever ailed them. It must have been devastating to be so close from season to season only to have someone else step down into the pool before him. He managed to get to the pool, but he could not get in it. Though there may have been others there who could assist, success was reserved for those who could get there first. If you weren't first you were last, and second place meant no healing. It wasn't only his own affliction that stood in the way of his healing. It was also the selfishness, self-centeredness and lack of concern of others that stood in his way. No one made it a priority to help him get in the water. No one assisted in positioning him to receive healing. Others had to ensure they (or their loved ones) made it into the water first.

God's Invasion

The man had been ill for 38 years. Though we don't know how long or how often he came to the pool, his disappointment had been consistent enough to alter his perspective. Maybe he began to view his life through the filter of *what was not happening* and *what he wasn't able to do.* It can be a dangerous perspective from which to view life. It creates an *"It's never like you imagine it"* mindset, which can wreak havoc on us mentally and emotionally.

It is a view of life that finds great disappointment when events and people don't meet preconceived expectations—whether those expectations are reasonable or unreasonable. It is a view that may be unwilling to adapt and reorient. Instead it wallows in *what should have or could have been.* It often causes us to avoid setting goals or having expectations because we are likely to think, *"It'll never happen anyway."* The reason the mindset is dangerous is because it has the potential to facilitate in us a chronic hopelessness. That hopelessness can overshadow the quality moments that occur in our lives as well as hinder our ability to dream faith-filled dreams.

Enter . . . the Lamb of God who takes away the sin of the world (John 1:29). Jesus already knew the man had been afflicted a long time. His question was, *"Do you wish to get well?"* Why that question? Of course he wants to get well—he *is* waiting by the pool. The man's response highlights a significant gap. His answer should have been YES—absolutely! Instead, his reply is a description of his circumstances: *I try to get there but nobody helps me.* Jesus already knew his circumstances.

How often do we want something from God, yet instead of asking for what we desire we bring Him a description of our circumstances? We explain our struggles, instead of saying, "Lord, heal me!" It is not my goal to suggest in any way that God isn't interested in hearing about our circumstances and struggles. I think as a loving Father, He is certainly interested and will patiently listen to us. He wants us to share our hearts and discuss with Him what we are feeling. The point I want to make, however, is that our prayers often end there.

God is intimately acquainted with our circumstances—He has known them since before the foundation of the world. He is *all knowing* and *all-powerful*. He doesn't need a description of our circumstances. He wants to hear the desires of our heart spoken in faith. Jesus' response to the man instructs him to *take action*. Jesus could have sat down and explained that He understood the situation, the severity of the affliction, the apparent selfishness of others and the depth of his despair. Yes, He understood every detail of the circumstances. However, the greater issue was what the Father was doing in the moment. Jesus focused on what He saw the Father doing. He saw the Father healing this man—even on the Sabbath. He heard the Father say, *"Get up, pick up your pallet and walk,"* so that is what Jesus said. There would always be time to reflect on the depth of an affliction and ruminate over the selfishness of others. This wasn't that time. God came to make his situation beautiful—not have him wallow in the details of it.

We, too, should be careful to not allow the despair of our circumstances to pervert and distort our perspective. It can cause us to miss what God wants to do in our lives *in a moment.* It is especially important if you live with pain or disappointment on what seems a recurring basis. The Devil will be quick to commend an *"It's never like you imagine it"* mindset. He wants you to live in hopelessness and despair especially if you name Christ as Savior. Satan wants you to believe God has abandoned you and that you aren't a priority with Him. Don't believe the lie! God has granted us the power of His Spirit and the creative gift of our own words to pray and speak life over our darkest situations. The words we speak should be His Word echoing in and rising from our hearts.

In Isaiah 43:26 God tells us to remind Him of His Word and state our case before Him. God needs no rehashing of the failures of those around us or play-by-play descriptions of their contributions to our plight. Our case must be stated on the basis of Jesus' obedience unto death—the righteousness of Christ and the efficacy of His blood to cleanse our sin. He does not need a blow-by-blow account of the consistent disappointment we have faced. Again, He cares about all of that because it touches our lives. However, what He wants from you and me is faith-filled acknowledgment of His power to save, deliver and keep us in spite of our situations. What He wants from us is a level of faith that reflects the depth of our love and the trust we have in Him.

6

God Has Invaded Our World

But when the fullness of the time came, God sent forth
His Son, born of a woman, born under the Law, so that
He might redeem those who were under the Law, that we
might receive the adoption as sons. Because you are sons,
God has sent forth the Spirit of His Son into our hearts,
crying, " Abba! Father!" Therefore you are no longer a
slave, but a son; and if a son, then an heir through God.
(Galatians 4:4-7 NASB)

God has invaded our world, and we are forever changed and made beautiful because of it. It doesn't matter where we come from or what we've been through. We don't have to live on the periphery of life. We are Kingdom dwellers who continually live in the presence of God. Our life and choices should reflect a Kingdom habitation. Embrace your part of the legacy. While the world may continue to define us by our circumstances, shortcomings, and inadequacies, God does not.

New Creations

Second Corinthians 5:17 reminds us *we are new creations in Christ Jesus; old things have passed away—new things have come.* Our old circumstances and situations should no longer define our existence or potential. God has invaded our existence—He is *Immanuel,* God with us. We are forever changed because of our encounter with Him. We have been rescued from the kingdom of darkness and transferred into the Kingdom of His Son (Colossians 1:13). Because we have a new habitation, we possess the potential to influence our environment in a very different way. Because of Christ Jesus, we have peace with God (Romans 5:1). There is no more enmity. Fear of retribution should *not* characterize our relationship with God. We are His workmanship created for good works (Ephesians 2:10).

Another important fact to remember about God's invasion of our world is that it is rarely *only* about us. When God invades our world, it is always about how all of His actions toward us impact our lives and the lives of those who are around us. God loves community, and much of what He does in our lives is done within the context of community— even when it appears it's just about an individual. In each of the lives we have looked at in this part of the book we see God's invasion impacting not only that person but their legacy as well.

In Rahab's life, we see God's invasion impacting the lineage of the Messiah. In Hannah's life, we see God's invasion impacting Israel's future leadership—both the office of the Prophet and the office of the King. When we see God invade Zechariah and Elizabeth's lives, we see Him preparing a platform for the one who will become the forerunner of the Messiah. When God invades the blind man's world, He strategically positions him to provide insight for those who were blind in the region— who were waiting for the Messiah and needed to know God cared.

So, how do we respond when God invades our world? How should we respond when our situations look hopeless, and God opens the door to hope? How do we respond when He gives us a glimpse of what could be?

Responding to God's Invasion . . .

Embrace an accurate perception of God. Rahab opened her head and her heart to *believe* the God of Israel could do something in her life for which there was no precedent. All she knew was what she heard of the mighty exploits He had accomplished among the nations. As God invaded her world, her choice was simple—she could place her trust in Him or live in hopelessness. Deep within her heart, Rahab must have believed that this God the Israelites talked about was so much more than she had ever experienced in her life.

The first decision Rahab made was to embrace an accurate perception of the God of Israel. As she embraced that accurate perception of Him, her faith was encouraged. Rahab opened her head and heart to the possibility God could do something her life that seemed impossible. She risked believing the God of Israel would be responsive to her faith in the same way He responded to His people. If no one else in Jericho understood what was happening, she certainly did. To everyone else in Jericho His name provoked a dreadful fear. In Rahab, however, word of the Hebrew God provoked a holy reverence and awe that translated into *faith*.

Don't allow your circumstances to change your testimony. The Shunammite was able to say, *"All is well!"* Even though she had a dead son lying on the guest bed in an upper room of her home. She held on to her testimony! She did not allow the circumstances to change what she knew to be true. She was able to declare, *"All is well"* because she understood that the same God who had blessed her with this great miracle child also possessed the power to raise the child from the dead. Both biblical history and empirical evidence remind us that we will experience trials in this life. Jesus Himself reminds us of this in John's gospel.

> "These things I have spoken to you, so that in Me you may have peace. In the world you have tribulation, but take courage; I have overcome the world." (John 16:33 NASB)

The Shunammite acknowledged the reality of the situation she was experiencing. At the same time, she did not allow this temporal experiential reality to change her testimony. *She had held the truth of God's words in her hands.* She had nursed him as an infant. She had dried his tears. She had rocked him to sleep. She knew what her *true testimony* was. It was a living, breathing son who was a gift from the Lord. Though her eyes saw the limp body of a dead youth lying in her lap, it did not change her testimony.

I encourage you, too, to hold on to your testimony. Do not allow circumstances and situations to alter your understanding of the truth. Continue in faith to pray for your marriages, your children, your friends, your jobs and any other situations that require your tenacity. God is for you! He is on your side. He will not abandon or fail you. He will not mislead or deceive you. Trust Him!

Fully Commit To Thriving. Engage the life God has given you. Our sanctification is worked out in the trenches of life. Our refinement and sharpening take place as we walk out the details of our lives. *Stop sitting around wishing your life was something else or that you were someone else.* This is the life you have, and it is a blessing as long as God is in it with you. It is up to you to make the most of it. We have the privilege every day to fully commit to and engage the lives we've been given. The people who are a part of our day-to-day lives aren't there by accident. The jobs we have did not come about by chance. The people we call family, friends and community are in our lives because God deems that each one of them is necessary for our refinement in order to bring Him glory.

The Scripture tells us to work out our salvation with fear and trembling (Philippians 2:12-13). As believers we have been saved, we are being saved and we will be saved. If we have read the Bible often enough we know the end of the story. We know we have victory in Christ Jesus. We know we have eternal life because of Christ Jesus. At this point, all that is left is for us to continue to walk out *what we say we believe* and live the life that He has given us in order to bring Him glory.

PART 3

He Makes All Things Beautiful By Giving Us Beauty Secrets for Life

Beauty secrets for life refers to the truths we hold close to our hearts which help us stay the course for God's glory. Most often, they are the truths we read in God's Word that take root in our hearts as we realize they are for us. God wants to bless us, protect us, keep and preserve us.

At other times, they are very personal words spoken deep within our hearts by Holy Spirit as God encourages us in the journey. They may come as a timely encouragement from a friend when we most need it. These personal words can often serve as the clarion call God uses to arrest our attention when it is our tendency is to wander off.

A regimen for authentic beauty . . .

A few years ago, Warner Brothers Pictures released the animated feature, *Hoodwinked*.[17] The story revolves around the antics of a few familiar fairytale characters mixed up in a crime and how each of them interpreted the details of the crime from a different perspective.

Each perspective was distorted because it lacked information about the *whole story.*

I think the definition of beauty as suffered the same demise. We've been hoodwinked for years. The varying viewpoints regarding beauty have distorted the definition of authentic beauty. As a result, we buy, try, fry and dye with no restrictions or limitations. Don't misunderstand me. I'm not opposed to the processes we engage in to enhance (or augment) our beauty. *I make my own systematic contributions to the cosmetic industry.* If, however, our doing so is an attempt to find true *beauty that* is acceptable by the world's standards, we're setting ourselves up for repeated failure and disappointment.

There is, however, a beauty regimen that is timeless in its application and *manageable* for all of us. Some may struggle with the word *regimen.* The word conjures up images of something rigid and harsh. I hope, however, you'll choose to view it as a useful word. I hope you'll allow it to speak to a plan and strategy for restoring and preserving an important aspect of who you are. Our *regimen* won't be measured by the numbers on a scale, the amount of gray hair we have, or whether the latest fashion trends compliment our figure. It will emphasize a beauty that emanates from within. Peter refers to it specifically in his first epistle:

> Your adornment must not be merely external—braiding the hair, and wearing gold jewelry, or putting on dresses; but let it be the hidden person of the heart, with the perishable quality of a gentle and quiet spirit, which is precious in the sight of God. (1 Peter 3:3-4 NASB)

While it's obvious Peter appreciates the role of outer beauty, these verses give us a view of *an inner beauty that shapes our outward behavior and demeanor.* The word *adornment* is the Greek word *kosmos.* The word refers to the world, with its primary meaning being order, regular disposition and arrangement.[18] In other words, let your world—*your order, regular disposition and arrangement*—be a mild, grace-filled and undisturbed kind of place. Our regular posture before the Lord and the world should be such that our personal world is steady, still and quiet inside. What does this mean for us? Chaos may break loose around us. World economic systems may be on the brink of collapse. Enemies may set up camp to torment and oppress from every side. Loved ones may be insensitive, and children can bounce off of the walls. In the midst of all of that, our inner climate is calm and centered on the One who made the universe.

So, how do we get there? Our lives aren't perfect, but they are being *perfectly shaped* and designed by a loving Father. There are strategies that can help us achieve an enduring beauty. They can undo the damage of the years behind us and keep us strong and resilient for the decades ahead. Like any sound beauty regimen, it begins with deep cleansing . . . .

Hold that thought! Before we move forward . . . .

If you have arrived at this point in the book, and it occurs to you that you don't fully understand all that has been said about *relationship* with God, *intimacy* with Him and *knowing* Him, it is time for me to pause. Before I talk about cleansing as a beauty secret for life and offer you principles to help you in your day-to-day living, I want to address everyone's need for the *ultimate cleansing*.

I'm referring to a cleansing that is available only by the blood of Jesus. It is the acknowledgment and acceptance of the truth that we are sinners—we are born into that sin. God created a perfect world—*in the beginning.* He gave man dominion over everything that existed— plants, trees, animals, beasts of the field and even creeping and crawling creatures. When God placed man in the garden, He gave him only one stipulation: he was not to eat from the tree of the knowledge of good and evil. God's warning was clear that death would be the result if man ate. Man's original sin ushered in death for all of mankind (Romans 5:12). However, even at the beginning, God was prepared with a plan of redemption to draw us back to relationship with Him. He does and has always desired to dwell among us—to live in our midst. He longs for relationship with us. Everything He does is about drawing us closer to Him. Everything He does is about being with us because He loves us.

From the very beginning, God had a plan of redemption that He was prepared to execute in order to reconcile us to Him. I don't know who you are or how you came across this book. I do know it is His will for you to know Him. He is not some distant, far-off God who doesn't care about you. He isn't sitting on His throne waiting for you to do wrong and hoping that His lightning bolt will strike your butt at just the right angle. *That isn't who He is!* He is a loving God who cares about every aspect of your life. He loves you so much He sent His Son to die on the cross for you (John 3:16). The blood Christ shed at Calvary is sufficient to satisfy the debt we incurred because of our sin—death. The Scripture makes it clear that the wages of sin is death—the payment for our sin should be death, and, in fact, it is (Romans 3:23). However, Romans 3:24 goes on to say, *". . . the gift of God is eternal life through Jesus Christ our Lord."*

In Christ, we have access to life—*life eternal*. In Christ, we are cleansed of the sin that separates us from a loving and holy God. In Christ, there is intimacy with God. So, as you prepare to read this section about being cleansed deeply in order to live an authentic beauty before the Lord, I would do you a disservice if I didn't first say to you, *"You must be born again."* So as not to overwhelm you, I'll keep the next steps simple. Pray in this direction:

Acknowledge you're a sinner and you need God's forgiveness. Accept the free gift of salvation God offers in Christ Jesus. (Romans 3:23-24; 5:5-8)

Believe that Christ lived a sinless life, died on the cross for your sin, and rose again and is seated at the right hand of God. (1 Corinthians 15: 3-4)

Confess Christ Jesus as Savior and Lord. Commit your heart to Him. (Romans 10:9-13)

If you prayed from your heart, welcome to the family! Now, let's move forward . . . .

7

Cleanse Deeply

Cleansers wash away surface dirt and anything else that covers or clings to our skin. The goal is to leave skin feeling clean and prepare it for any other applications that may be part of our beauty regimen. Applying this concept is necessary for our lives and hearts as well. The washing of our lives with the Word of God removes the dirt we acquire as we walk out our faith. We live in a fallen world—a world impacted by sin and polluted by evil. It's naive of us to think we won't be tainted or jaded by it in some way. We live in a 24-hour information culture. Daily, we rub up against mindsets and ideas that run counter to the truths we believe. Let's face it. Sometimes stuff sticks!

At the same time, we are called to be *salt and light* in this fallen world. God's intent is for us to *bring His flavor* to the mix and to *repel the darkness.* We are cities set on a hill that can't be hid. We're not to be lights under a bushel. Instead, we let our light shine for people in such a way that it gives the world the correct opinion of our God. (Matthew 5:13-14) *Cleansing is an intentional process.* It implies I must be willing to remove those things that have the potential to dim my light or keep me from shining brightly.

Be willing to let the Word work you over

> For the word of God is living and active, sharper than any two-edged sword, piercing to the division of soul and of spirit, of joints and of marrow, and discerning the thoughts and intentions of the heart. (Hebrews 4:12 ESV)

Years ago I met someone who consciously chose not to spend time reading her Bible. She would often talk about the challenges she experienced and how she wanted change. She professed to know Christ as Savior, so one day I decided to ask why she didn't read her Bible. Her response was enlightening: *"Because whenever I read it, I see myself in it!"*

Frankly, it's the best excuse I've ever heard for not reading it! I think she was absolutely right—*and that's the point.* When we expose ourselves to God's Word, we see ourselves in it. We see our sinfulness and depravity. If we look into it long and hard enough, however, we will also see God's mercy, grace and love being poured out all over us.

The error many of us make is we assume God is attempting (like some angry boss or parent) to catch us doing something wrong. That isn't His goal. His is a plan of redemption and reconciliation! He is helping us get it right, so we can get back to Him. May I encourage you to stop viewing Him as some great punisher who is looking for retribution regarding your heinous sin? Try seeing Him for who He is—a loving, holy, powerful God who adores you because He chooses to love you.

Be willing to expose yourself to the Word of God. It is vital and powerful. It will expose motives and reveal intentions. With the precision of a fine sword it will cut away layers of emotional and mental junk. When that happens, DON'T RUN! The same two-edged sword will also provide the healing you need as the light of God's Word shines on those areas of vulnerability. Embrace the process and receive His healing.

Pursue knowledge of God

> For Ezra had set his heart to study the law of the LORD and
> to practice it, and to teach His statutes and ordinances in
> Israel. (Ezra 7:10 NASB)

Ezra was a man skilled at what he did—he was a scribe. He was skilled in the Law of Moses and favored by God . . . whose hand was upon him (Ezra 7:6). Ezra *set his heart to study the law of the Lord.* The Hebrew word for *set* is a verb meaning to *set up, to make firm, to establish, to prepare.* The primary action of this verb is to cause to stand in an upright position, and thus the word also means *fixed* or *steadfast.*[19] Ezra narrowed his attention and focused his heart on studying the law of the Lord so he could *do it* and *teach it.* His level of commitment was necessary for his leadership role in Israel. While he had been blessed with the necessary skill set as well as God's favor, he still had to *make a decision to set his heart to study.*

Many of us can relate to having to make tough decisions about the effective use of our time. I've been working on a few major projects that have taken far too long to complete. The reason they weren't complete was because I hadn't focused my attention or dedicated the time necessary to see them through. Once I made the decision to do some things differently, many of the pieces came together and obstacles were overcome. I've been encouraged by the major strides I've been able to make, but it began with making a quality choice to fix my attention on what mattered.

The fact is we can't do everything all of time—we must make choices. Ideally, we seek the Lord's guidance regarding direction and priorities. We keep things in proper order when we trust His leading. Like Ezra, I want to consistently set my heart to study God's Word. I love that Ezra was able to stay focused. Talent and gifting can sometimes be distracting. We can sometimes forget that everything we have comes from the Lord, and we can't do anything apart from Him (John 15:5). In the end, we want to steward well over every responsibility our heavenly Father entrusts to us and be found intentionally and purposefully doing God's will.

Ezra didn't allow his ability or standing with God to diminish his diligence to study. I wonder how often we let our talent, skill and ability get in the way of what God wants to do in our lives? Sometimes, we rest on our laurels. Sure, the talent is from the Lord, but we should still be diligent to *do* and *teach*—with our lives. Ezra was *fixed* in the deepest part of who he was. He made himself a *student* of the Law as well as a *teacher* to others. He is a powerful model for those of us who would teach as well.

Be intentional and purposeful to establish times to study and meditate on God's Word. I can't presume to know what a typical day is like for you, but sometimes my days resemble organized chaos. There occasionally emerges some semblance of order and by day's end I can be exhausted. I have even struggled with making time to write this book. I had to finally decide to weave it into the daily fabric of my life and use the process for my own spiritual growth.

Becoming beautiful means pursuing the right things at the right time. It means pursuing an accurate knowledge of who God is and how great His love is for us. Our deep cleansing begins here because it is God's desire to be known by us. He has been intentional about creating opportunities for us to dwell in His presence. It is His presence that cleanses. It is His Word that washes us. This is a critical process in our lives if it is our true desire to be authentically beautiful.

Purify your thought life

> For though we walk in the flesh, we do not war according
> to the flesh, for the weapons of our warfare are not of

the flesh, but divinely powerful for the destruction of
fortresses. We are destroying speculations and every lofty
thing raised up against the knowledge of God, and we are
taking every thought captive to the obedience of Christ.
(2 Corinthians 10:3-6 NASB)

I don't want to over simplify this point, but the bottom line is that
we must become *masters* at roping in and controlling our thought life.
We need to be proactive about destroying speculations and making every
thought we have *bow in submission* to the truth of God's Word. The word
speculation means to *reckon, calculate, consider, or reflect.*[20] I love these
words! This Scripture makes it clear that our reckonings, considerations,
reflections and calculations will endeavor to usurp authority against
the truth of God's Word. Therefore, we must be in a constant state of
destroying those thought processes that run counter to God's truth.

If we aren't diligent, we will find ourselves trapped and bound in
a cycle of destruction that will constantly disrupt our lives. In case
you're wondering if it's really that big a deal . . . . Think about the last
argument you had—*in your mind*—with a participant who wasn't even
present. I'm sure you did a masterful job at telling them off with a sharp
one-liner that cut 'em to bits. You let them let know who's who and
what's what! The problem is . . . they weren't really there. You crafted the
whole dialogue in your mind. You allowed one *thought* to build upon
another until the entire screenplay developed. When the credits rolled
and the theme music played, your name was in lights. Now, before you
accept the award for best actor/actress in a dramatic life-changing role,
reflect on what thought should have been taken captive early in the dialogue.
That's the point at which we must take authority over Satan's tactics to
destroy our lives.

The more *consistent* we become at taking thoughts captive, the
less often we'll find ourselves being enslaved by the stories we tell

ourselves—stories which create emotional turmoil and physical discomfort. When we refuse to bring thoughts captive to the obedience of Christ, we position ourselves to be ensnared by lies and distortions, which seek to destroy our souls.

I, personally, find this to be the most challenging hurdle I face on the road to spiritual maturity. Long before my words or actions cause harm to others, it is my thought life that must be controlled. If it is out of the abundance of the heart that the mouth speaks (Matthew 12:34, Luke 6:45), then my words are merely a reflection of the *context of my thoughts.* My murmuring, carping and whining are the outward symptoms of thoughts and musings that have not bowed in submission to the authority of God. I can make all sorts of excuses for why this happens. In the end it's about poor choices I make that impact the quality of my life.

My deep cleansing requires I make every thought that crosses my mind bow in submission to God's Word. It means I have to put my foot on the neck of speculations, reckonings and reflections that don't align with God's Word. I wish I could do this once in my life and be done with it forever, but that just isn't the case. This, like most cleansing in our life, requires constant vigilance. I have to do this *daily.* I have to do it *frequently.* I have to do it *consistently.* Being intentional in this area really does help to purify my thought life and remove the debris that would serve to mar the beauty God intends for me.

> You are already clean because of the word which I have spoken to you. "Abide in Me, and I in you. As the branch cannot bear fruit of itself unless it abides in the vine, so neither *can* you unless you abide in Me. "I am the vine, you are the branches; he who abides in Me and I in him, he bears much fruit, for apart from Me you can do nothing. (John 15:3-5 NASB)

Guard your heart

> Watch over your heart with all diligence, for from it flow the springs of life. (Proverbs 4:23 NASB)

As the parent of a *rapidly* growing and inquisitive child, the number of questions kids can ask amazes me. Even more amazing are the conclusions they derive based on what is sometimes limited information from obscure sources. It is a reminder to me of the need to guard my heart from those things that come to steal dreams, distort perceptions and twist mindsets. It's our heart that becomes the storehouse for all things wonderful. We must guard it from *toxins,* which aim to move us from the path God has for us. Proverbs 4:23 is preceded by nuggets of wisdom that emphasize the focus of a Father's words to his son. The wise son keeps them deep in his heart because they give life and health to those who find them. The verses that follow instruct the son to put away a deceitful mouth, fix the gaze of his eyes and keep his feet on a straight path (Proverbs 4:24-27). I think that'll preach, and the sermon would be short:

> **"Stay in the Word. Guard your heart. Watch your mouth.
> Be careful what you see, and stay on the path. Amen!"**

Our heart is a key indicator of how we're doing. First John 3:21-22 reminds us if our hearts don't condemn us, we have peace with God. How we've previously handled our thought life significantly impacts how much war we wage to guard our hearts. Please don't be lulled into thinking you can compartmentalize destructive thought processes and not have them impact the resources within you from which flow the issues of life. It isn't realistic or doable. As human beings, we aren't great at that kind of multi-tasking or *double-mindedness.*

Here's a word picture to help clarify my point: I've always been a bit tickled by the preference some people have that their food items not touch each other when they are on a plate. I always think to myself, *"Once you swallow, all of your food items will touch each other!"* The same is true of our thought life and our heart. There is no way to keep them from touching and blending together. Everything we think, reflect on and ponder has the potential to touch our heart and every other area of our lives as well. There is no getting around it. We must stop living lives where we act as though what we do on Thursday will not impact the quality of life we experience on Monday.

Every encounter we experience engages our hearts and minds. It's an area many of us take far too lightly. Perhaps, it never occurs to us that everything we experience and permit in our lives could have some sort of impact on us. The truth, however, is that unless we are intentional about pursuing knowledge of God and purifying our thought life, it may not even occur to us that we need to guard our hearts. Like some, we might think *"It doesn't matter; It's just not that big a deal."* Beloved, that is the lie the Enemy of our souls wants us to believe. The tactics of the Devil are the same as they were in the garden. He provokes us to question the validity of God's commands and counsel (Genesis 3:1). He distorts the truth and encourages our presumption to think we know more through our own reasoning. He caters to our fleshly lusts in hope they will draw us into intercourse with *lust and self*. When they have conceived, they bring forth sin (James 1:13-15). Don't be deceived—it's the same dog that still bites the same way!

Watch over your heart with all diligence, for from it flow the springs of life . . . .

8

Refine and Tone

Toners remove any remaining impurities that may still be present after cleansing. They typically have a few stronger ingredients within them: saline, alcohol, etc. These additions help remove the stubborn dirt and oils that clog the pores and promote blemishes. In the same way, we should always be looking deeper within ourselves to see what impurities remain. Are there secret sins that you don't even discuss with God? Are there secret fears which have you bound and terrified? Remember that nothing is too difficult for God (Jeremiah 32:17). Eliminate the clutter in your life, remain hungry and teachable and pursue excellence in Him.

Eliminate clutter and pursue clarity

Therefore, since we have so great a cloud of witnesses surrounding us, let us also lay aside every encumbrance and the sin which so easily entangles us, and let us run with endurance the race that is set before us, fixing our eyes on Jesus, the author and perfecter of faith, who for the joy set before Him endured the cross, despising the shame, and has sat down at the right hand of the throne of God. For consider Him who has endured such hostility by sinners against Himself, so that you will not grow weary and lose heart. (Hebrews 12:1-3 NASB)

These verses follow the famous hall of fame of faith in Hebrews 11. The writer of Hebrews now encourages us on the basis of this great cloud of witnesses who have gone before us. They are witnesses who endured difficult circumstances, rose above unfortunate beginnings and overcame flimsy excuses. They, by the grace of God, talked the talk and walked the walk. Because of the road they walked and the testimonies they left behind, we, too, can look to Jesus—the Author and Finisher of our faith.

Jesus is the Initiator of our faith, and He will see us through to the end. His endurance of the cross is the strength and encouragement we must embrace in order to run this race. Our focus on Christ and insight regarding those who've gone before us will help us eliminate the clutter that seeks to dominate our lives. When we focus on Jesus, we gain the clarity we need to keep our vision clear.

Remain hungry and teachable

How blessed is the man who does not walk in the counsel of the wicked, nor stand in the path of sinners, nor sit in the seat of scoffers! But his delight is in the law of the LORD, and in His law he meditates day and night. He will be like a tree firmly planted by streams of water, which yields its fruit in its season and its leaf does not wither; and in whatever he does, he prospers. (Psalm 1:1-3 NASB)

This my favorite Psalm. It contains awesome insights about refining and toning—those extra measures we take to remove impurities from our lives. In this case, it is about more than just reading God's Word—it is about growing to delight in it. How do we get there? The most obvious answer is to spend time in it. Keep in mind that *everything* in your life will war against this. The cares of this world—the trappings of this life—will compete for your attention in this area.

Our delight in His Word increases as we come to understand *who He is* through it. All of us might know someone who seems to know everything contained in Scripture. They can quote verses, provide background context for books of the Bible, and may even be able to tell you *Hebrew* and *Greek* origins of words. However, delighting in the Law of the Lord is about gaining an increasing understanding of *who He is*—His nature and His character. When we begin to do that, His Word becomes more than just a book we should make time to read every day. It connects us to Him in a special way and helps us know Him more. When we move toward delight, we can move away from fretting over whether devotion time should include 10 minutes, 10 verses or 10 chapters. When we flow in delight, every jot and tittle becomes priceless because it increases our awareness and understanding of who He is. Our intimacy with Him deepens. When we delight in His Word, we are delighting in Him. They are His words, His character and His nature on display. We are inclining toward Him, and He is drawing near to us.

There are seasons when staying committed is tough. One of my difficult seasons was during graduate school. I knew all of the right answers: God should be first, and His Word must have priority. Yet, I had so much information swirling around in my head I thought I'd overload and explode. In addition, I had been asked to be the key speaker at our annual women's retreat during my last year of school. I was honored by the invitation and wanted to do a great job. I felt completely overwhelmed. Though I was excited about my degree program, it bothered me that school was disrupting my routine. However, everything I learned better prepared me for every ministry opportunity with which I was confronted—including the retreat. I knew I had heard from the Lord that it was the right season to return to school. I also knew that some of my anguish was about my own lack of discipline.

In the end, I had to return to the truth of God's Word—delight and meditate. In the midst of the struggle, there was fruit. This book was born out of that season, as were many other opportunities to share my heart for God's Word. That season of *taking in* prepared me to *share* what God had placed within me. The retreat experience was amazing—I came home refreshed and energized! The renewed energy helped me finish graduate school. My schedule was cramped, and there were times when I wanted to quit. While I struggled with having to set aside a few responsibilities, in the end, it was the right thing to do. The volume in my head lowered, and I was able to be more tactically effective.

It was during that season I concluded *balance is an illusion*. Whenever I observe a set of *balanced scales*, there is also no movement. While that may be fine for a pair of scales, it does not work for me. My life doesn't fit into that frame. There is always movement in my life. Instead of trying to find balance, I've learned to *manage the movement* of my life. I try to be much more cognizant of my priorities and remain open to learning new things and being adaptive.

In the midst of managing all of this movement, I have also grown in my appreciation of the value of *stillness*. Jesus told Martha that Mary had chosen the *better thing* when she made the decision to sit at His feet versus run about making preparations here and there. There will always be a myriad of choices before us that seek to usurp the place of the better thing. The better thing will always be whatever it takes to remain close to Him. I confess that most days find me smacking around the Mini-Martha in me. I'm a *doer* by personality. I can be pretty *all over the place* if I'm not careful. I have to be intentional about narrowing my focus to the task at hand and following through to get things done. I do get a lot done, but I have to work at staying in my lane. It takes a tremendous effort to keep Mini-Martha still especially at the beginning of my day—the time I most enjoy personal devotion and study time in the Word.

Refining and toning requires that we look for what needs to be purged from our system. In order for that to happen, we have to chew on, muse over and ponder God's Word. The glow of authentic beauty is diminished when we lose our hunger for God's Word or aren't teachable. We will thrive, however, when our meditation is pure and we're poised to give liberally in those areas God desires.

Pursue excellence in Christ

> Seeing that His divine power has granted to us everything pertaining to life and godliness, through the true knowledge of Him who called us by His own glory and excellence. For by these He has granted to us His precious and magnificent promises, so that by them you may become partakers of the divine nature, having escaped the corruption that is in the world by lust. Now for this very reason also, applying all diligence, in your faith supply moral excellence, and in your moral excellence, knowledge, and in your knowledge, self-control, and in your self-control, perseverance, and in your perseverance, godliness, and in your godliness, brotherly kindness, and in your brotherly kindness, love. For if these qualities are yours and are increasing, they render you neither

useless nor unfruitful in the true knowledge of our Lord
Jesus Christ. (2 Peter 1:3-8 NASB)

God has already bestowed on us everything that pertains to living a
godly life. We have access to everything we need to live out a victorious,
faith-filled and overcoming life. It's obtained and maintained through
a *true knowledge* of Him. Pursuing a true knowledge of God requires
diligence on our part. It's more than *head knowledge* of God. It's a *heart
knowledge* that I allow to impact the way I live. It means spending time
with God in prayer, being quiet, reading the Word, gathering with other
believers and sharing His love with others.

Peter also makes it clear that we have a responsibility to be very
intentional about growing in His presence. He is instructing us to
do our very best—give our best effort—at excelling in seven specific
areas. The first is moral excellence. We are to work on being people of
excellent character and integrity. Peter knows we are saved by grace
through faith. This is not about earning salvation brownie points with
God. This is about reflecting moral character that gives the world the
correct opinion of who God is—even when no one else is looking. It
is about being honest with ourselves regarding our vulnerabilities and
shortcomings and allowing God to reshape and mold us to reflect the
image of Christ (Romans 8:29).

We are to add to our moral excellence, knowledge. We must *know*
Him and always desire to *know* Him more. If you have been tracking
with me up to this point, you know this means time in His Word and
in His presence. It means meditating, musing over and reflecting on
His truth.

To knowledge, we add self-control. Yes, God used the word *self*. We
are to control ourselves. We cannot hope someone else will keep us from
behaving badly. Our family can't do it. Our friends can't do it. Our

pastors can't do it. *We* (you and I) must choose to control ourselves—our behavior, our mouths, our thoughts. *No one else is causing us to behave badly, throw tantrums, have fits, or act like spiritual brats.* We make those choices when we abandon self-control. We make those choices when we exalt our desire and will above God's will. The last time I checked, that pattern of behavior never yields positive results.

> How can a young man keep his way pure? By keeping *it* according to Your word. (Psalm 119:9 NASB)

For years, as I considered this verse, I envisioned God placing a protective hedge around us to keep us pure. In fact, I have prayed for this protective hedge around myself and those I love based on my understanding of this passage. However, sometime last year, I was digging a little deeper and realized that while God will place a hedge of protection around us, He also calls us to *guard ourselves* based on the truths of His Word. He has given us the capacity to make quality choices—choices that add value and bring refreshing to our lives. *Self-control is about making the best choices in the moment.*

We add to self-control, perseverance. Essentially, we hang in there. We keep in mind that the challenges we face now will seem light in comparison to what awaits us. We focus on the fact that endurance must be allowed to perfect its work in us (James 1:4).

> Therefore we do not lose heart, though our outer man is decaying, yet our inner man is being renewed day by day. For momentary, light affliction is producing for us an eternal weight of glory far beyond all comparison, while we look not at the things which are seen, but at the things which are not seen; for the things which are seen are temporal, but the things which are not seen are eternal. (2 Corinthians 4:16-18 NASB)

What an encouraging word from the Lord. Do not get discouraged. Do not lose heart. God calls our present situations and circumstances *momentary light afflictions.* To the degree that we keep that perspective, we do a much better job of navigating our *valley experiences.* I can share that my greatest challenges are usually connected to my inability or unwillingness to look at *the things that are not seen.* Whenever I struggle, it is because my eyes are on what I can see—they are not on the spiritual. Because I am temporally focused, I invite anxiety, fretting and despair to pull up a chair and get on my last nerve! My choices have made them welcomed guests. However, this isn't God's best for me. In order to persevere, I have to maintain my spiritual focus.

As we persevere, we add godliness. We reflect God's character. We do this by opening His Word and yielding ourselves to being conformed to the image of Christ (Romans 8:29). We say what He says, and we do what He does. It means laying down our will in exchange for His desire. It may also mean letting go of things that no longer add value to our lives.

To godliness, we add brotherly kindness. God calls us to encourage one another and be kind hearted toward one another. It means considering how our actions will impact the lives of those around us. We pay attention to the words we use and how we speak to others. We make choices that profit not only us but those with whom we're in relationship with as well. Lastly, we are to love. I will address this more in the next chapter. At this point, it is important for us to remember Jesus' words regarding the greatest commandment:

> And He said to him, " 'You shall love the Lord your God with all your heart, and with all your soul, and with all your mind.' "This is the great and foremost commandment. "The second is like it, 'You shall love your neighbor as yourself.'

"On these two commandments depend the whole Law and the Prophets. (Matthew 22:37-40 NASB)

If all of these qualities: *moral excellence, knowledge, self-control, perseverance, godliness, brotherly kindness, and love* are continually increasing, then we can add value in every situation we encounter. God promises we will be *fruitful* and *useful*. We have been saved by grace through faith in Christ (Ephesians 2:8). This salvation is a priceless gift from our Heavenly Father. God is emphasizing here, however, the point that we have acquired a great responsibility with this *so great salvation* we have received. There is nothing we have to do to earn or work for it. God gives us these instructions because our efforts in these areas impact and enhance the quality of life we live before others and the quality of service we render in His Kingdom.

9

Moisturize

C leansers wash away, toners evaporate, but moisturizer is intended to remain in place to hydrate and protect. It often includes blockers to prevent sun damage and contributes to a more youthful look. The real benefit of a moisturizer is that it helps provide and maintain suppleness in our skin. It's a great parallel for our own need to remain pliable and adaptive in God's presence.

The key here is *love*. Christ told His disciples that He was leaving them with two Commandments: Love God and Love People *(my translation of Matthew 22:37-39)*. By far, they are the most challenging pursuits we have as believers. When the Pharisees came to Jesus reminding Him Moses allowed them to give a certificate of divorce, he reminded them that Moses did so because of the *hardness of their hearts*. The word implies *"destitution of spiritual perception."*[21] The analogy is profound. When our spiritual perception is off, we become hard, calloused and brittle. Jesus' rebuke was about more than divorce; it was about a *spiritual myopia* that had occurred within the people.

my•o•pia \mī-ˈō-pē-ə\ *noun*

> **1:** a condition in which the visual images come to a focus in front of the retina of the eye resulting especially in defective vision of distant objects
>
> **2:** a lack of foresight or discernment: a narrow view of something—**my•o•pic** \-ˈō-pik,—ˈä-\ adjective[22]

It isn't my intention to be insensitive to anyone who is experiencing (or has experienced) separation or divorce. Jesus made it clear divorce certificates were *the outward sign of the loss of an inward spiritual perception.* They also represented the narrowing of attention to circumstances and details that were immediate and closest to them. As such, long-term spiritual vision was skewed and defective. Hardness of heart had choked off the channel for love. Consequently, their mindsets were calloused and brittle. They had lost sight of the sanctity and purpose of marriage—to reflect God's glory.

This is what happens when we refuse to love or when our love grows cold. Despite how spiritually adept we believe we are, our vision is distorted. Our foresight and discernment can be hindered because we've erected obstacles that block our sight. This is why this *spiritual moisturizer* is so important. So how do we remain pliable and adaptive in the hands of a creative and loving God?

Remember to love

> But when the Pharisees heard that Jesus had silenced the Sadducees, they gathered themselves together. One of them, a lawyer, asked Him *a question,* testing Him, "Teacher, which is the great commandment in the Law?" And He said to him, " 'You shall love the Lord your God with all your

heart, and with all your soul, and with all your mind.' "This is the great and foremost commandment. "The second is like it, 'You shall love your neighbor as yourself.' "On these two commandments depend the whole Law and the Prophets." (Matthew 22:34-40 NASB)

Love God . . . love people! I have to remind myself of this number one (and two) rule often. God's love has been poured out in our hearts (Romans 5:5). We have been equipped with the capacity to love. We have a responsibility to pour that love on others. No matter what happens in our lives, we are to endeavor to love. Love is both *preemptive* and *preventive* in its impact. When it flows and grows, as it should, it drives away bitterness and hardness of heart. Love keeps us tender and pliable. It helps us flex and adapt to new situations. It is an *action* we take as well as a byproduct of our actions toward others. Love keeps us beautiful in all of the ways that matter.

Remember Jesus' reflection on these two Commandments, *"on these hang all the Law and the prophets."* All of the Law and the teachings of the prophets are summarized in these two Commandments. Every point made in the Word of God, every adventure, every struggle, every victory should move us toward obeying these two commandments: Love God, love people. It is instructive to us that the *expert in the Law* asks the question, *"Which is the greatest Commandment?"* From the perspective of the Pharisees and Sadducees, it would have been convenient for Jesus to answer, "just obey God and you will be good." This would have allowed them to go about their way fulfilling the requirements of the Law while overlooking the *spirit* and *intent* of it.

In addition to being our schoolmaster, the Law also provided an opportunity for man to demonstrate his devotion to God through his outward actions. If Jesus had responded, *"Just obey God"* they might have been content with adhering to the specifics of the Law. Jesus, however, responds with two Commandments. His requirement would be that we not only *love God with all of our heart soul, mind and strength,* but we must also *love people.* In doing so, He highlights that it isn't enough to do right toward God, we must also *do right toward those created by God and in His image.* We may lift our hands to heaven in worship toward God, but we must also extend our hands to others in demonstration of the love we have for them. For most of us, the *loving God* part may seem much easier. Loving people is where we end up working out our salvation with fear and trembling (Philippians 2:12).

I don't have any quick fix answers for how we learn to love more. I can, however, offer one thought. When you find it tough to love another, try to wrap your mind around how great the Savior's love is for you.

Remain thankful and grateful

> Let the word of Christ richly dwell within you, with all wisdom teaching and admonishing one another with psalms and hymns and spiritual songs, singing with thankfulness in your hearts to God. Whatever you do in word or deed, do all in the name of the Lord Jesus, giving thanks through Him to God the Father. (Colossians 3:16-17 NASB)

One way to remain pliable and flexible is to intentionally remain thankful and grateful. It is a critical element in our development as mature believers. What precedes giving thanks is our willingness to allow the Word of Christ to dwell—reside/take up residence—within us.[23] There is tremendous value in the *indwelling Word.* It continually refines our world view and purview in order to understand how to respond to the world around us. It is how Joseph was able to endure the long season of preparation that preceded his ascension to the position of Governor of Egypt.

In Genesis 50, we see Joseph's response to his brothers as they approached him in fear after their father's death. They presumed Joseph would seek revenge for all they had done to him. Joseph, however, acknowledged that God was at work in the situation making what was meant for evil, work for something good. I don't think his awareness of that truth occurred overnight. I suspect his perspective was seasoned and developed over time. During what should have been the toughest, driest seasons of his life, he was being promoted and elevated. After being sold into slavery, his outward behavior led to his promotion in Potiphar's house. After being falsely accused of attempted rape, he was wrongfully imprisoned. He was promoted with leadership responsibility over the other inmates because in the midst of the trial, he reflected God's glory—*gave everyone the correct opinion of God*. While in prison, he found favor with a baker and cupbearer. Along the way, there was an attitude of thanks that acknowledged God's presence with him. That attitude left room for Joseph to bring God tremendous glory.

An attitude of thankfulness and remembering to be grateful will also help us avoid the trap of *entitlement*. When we allow the Word of Christ to dwell richly within us, we have a built-in reminder to be grateful for everything we receive. It helps us avoid an *attitude of entitlement* that says, "*I deserve this because I behaved well as a Christian—I obeyed, I gave, I served.*"

Attitudes of thankfulness and gratefulness will also produce in us a very necessary humility. That humility will serve us well as it helps us remember the graciousness of God and the mercy He demonstrates toward us every day of our lives. Giving thanks and displaying gratitude in the midst of hardship, damaged emotions, or heartaches may not be easy or comfortable. It's important to remember that the same *loving God* who encourages us to respond this way, is also intimately acquainted with our hurts, disappointments and betrayals. He knows better than anyone else what it means to be deeply wounded inside by those you trust or expect to protect and support you.

Be patient with yourself

> For I am confident of this very thing, that He who began a
> good work in you will perfect it until the day of Christ Jesus.
> (Philippians 1:6 NASB)

Keeping this truth close to our hearts helps keep us pliable in the hands of God. When we are mindful of the fact God is at work in us and on our behalf, it helps us be patient with ourselves. The apostle Paul reminded the church at Philippi of the confidence he had that God would complete the work He had begun in them. We can live with the same confidence ourselves. God is at work in us—He hasn't given up on us! He desires that we reflect His glory and be vessels of righteousness. He has made a huge investment in us because He loved us.

Don't be quick to assume problems, challenges and trials are an indication of your failure or God's abandonment. Both Paul and James, the half brother of Jesus wrote that we are to rejoice when trials come because they have the unique purpose of producing endurance in us (James 1:2-3; Romans 5:3). *Our endurance is developed when our faith is tested*. We build endurance muscles when circumstances present themselves in such a way as to cause us to doubt God. Our commitment to stand in faith and hold fast to God's Word produces endurance. It makes our spiritual shoulders strong. We're able to bear up under the weight of conflicting circumstances and keep our faith stayed on the one who is its *Author* and *Perfecter* (Hebrews 12:2).

So, be patient with yourself. Settle in for a long adventurous journey with the Lord. I currently have the book, *A Long Obedience in the Same Direction*,[24] on my nightstand. The title drew me to the book. It brings to mind a picture of holding the Father's hand as I journey down the long road with Him. Being patient with ourselves helps us avoid the bitterness and frustration that results when we are not where we think we should be.

We are in the hands and heart of a loving God. We are His planting and we're being fashioned for His glory. He is perfecting every detail of our existence. This sometimes means He is pruning things off of us. At other times, He may be grafting things in. Our job is to stay deeply rooted and planted and allow Him to have His way. He understands better than anyone what fruit we're capable of producing. He knows how and which lives our fruit will impact. He simply asks us to trust Him and believe He will faithfully follow through on His Word.

10

Personal Beauty Secrets

My list certainly isn't exhaustive, but it contains a few of the secrets that have remained closest to my heart over the years. I suspect they've also been important because they represent the areas where I'm most prone to fail.

Learn to respond rather than react

I was a fairly new believer and was assigned to Kadena Air Base Okinawa. I was also a new instructor and excited about a new season of my career. We ran two 4-6 week courses at the professional military education center. Upon completion, all students received a graduation certificate while the top ten percent received special honors and recognition. At the end of one course, a disgruntled student accused me of showing preferential favor toward another student, which the student felt cost graduation recognition. Because I was new, I had not had any significant input into student feedback for the award process. The accusation, however, sent me into an emotional tailspin. I was hurt and wounded—all I wanted was to be a great instructor. It really bothered me that winning a class award could have meant so much that the student would make such an accusation.

My supervisor (and resident mentor) sent me away to dry my tears and calm down. He later discussed the scenario with me. After assuring me my credibility wasn't in question because of the student's accusation, he focused on what he considered the real issue—*my emotional reaction*. His words to me were simple: "Marv, you have to learn to respond rather than react." His theory was that *reacting required no real thought.* My reaction had been the emotional melt down he had witnessed behind a false accusation from a student. His goal in the meeting was to help me see the value of *thinking through and responding rationally* to what had occurred. Instead of responding based on what I knew to be true, I reacted to something I had no control over—the lie that came from someone else's mouth. I was so focused on what happened I overlooked the fact it was a lie in the first place.

That first lesson remains an important one for me. I'd like to tell you that since that day in the late 80s, I've mastered the ability to respond rather than react. Nothing would be further from the truth. I have, however, remembered the event and the lesson that followed. Learning to *own my responses* as I take thoughts captive still requires due diligence on my part. My supervisor's advice has become an important *beauty secret* for me. I can flashback to a few choice moments when it appeared I'd never been taught the lesson at all. But as I've already mentioned, it represents an area where I'm prone to blow it when I forget.

Stay Close to Him

I was invited to speak at a women's fellowship hosted by a seasoned minister in the congregation who was steady, quiet and had a deep love for God. It was one of my first opportunities to speak to a women's group. By this time, I was assigned to Tyndall Air Force Base Florida. Our Chapel family was a close knit group and very encouraging. Chaplain Herrie Reed was a *spiritual mentor* to me. I was in the nascent stages of learning to study the Bible. He encouraged my love for God's Word and was always pointing me to resources that would encourage me to grow.

I shared from the book of Esther. I had been so nervous as I prepared—I kept reading and re-reading Esther. Years later, I have grown to understand that was a very good thing. Even though I had been recognized as one of the best instructors in the Air Force, I didn't really know how to put together a formal message to speak at a church event. I held the Word in such high esteem, I was afraid to treat it as if I were building research for a training session. So, I read and re-read again. I wanted to know and understand the specifics of the account and allow Holy Spirit to tell me what to share.

When the day came to speak, I was overwhelmed by the way God poured out in our midst. The women were moved and hearts were touched. I was overwhelmed and so thankful to have been a part of such a blessed outpouring of His presence. Afterwards, our hostess prayed with me. Her counsel and encouragement were simple and straightforward: "*Stay close to Him.*" She kept her explanation simple and didn't embellish. I knew her words were important and intentional in that moment. I knew then as I know now that I was to hold on to those words. A few years ago as I was studying the Letter to the Hebrews and reflected on Hebrews 2:1,

> For this reason we must pay much closer attention to what
> we have heard, so that we do not *drift*[25] away from it.

According to Zodhiates, this is the only use of the word *parrero*, drift, in the Bible. It means to float or drift by as a river or ship.

Figuratively, it means to slip away, suggesting a gradual and almost unnoticed movement past a certain point.[26] I liken it to suddenly realizing I'm very far from where I should be but having no awareness that I was moving away. In those seasons when the cares of this world, busyness and other distractions pull me away or cause me to drift, I hear those words again—*stay close to Him*. It's the Master's call to me to make my way home in my heart and in my mind. It's His gentle reminder that causes me to assess my strategy for seeking Him in prayer, staying in His Word, or fellowshipping with His people—the Body of Christ. Since then, I have held those words close to my heart.

To this day, I consider it the best counsel I've ever received. They are words that steady me when busyness, distractions and anxiety attempt to trump the peace in my life. They are the trumpet call, which refocuses me when my own selfishness, self-centeredness and personal agenda cause me to wander away from the path to which God has called me. Perhaps, too, they are a reminder that His outpouring at the women's meeting wasn't about reading and re-reading as much as it was about the time spent with Him as I read. Because so much of my life is spent in *presentation or training mode*, it can become easy to think all I need are a few logical main points and sub points to make an impact during a training session or speaking engagement. Again, nothing could be further from the truth. It is my time in His presence, in His face, in His Word that has made the difference. *It will always be what makes the difference.*

So That You May Know That I AM God

It is one of my favorite encouragements from God's Word. It is often the answer to many of my "why" questions. From the beginning, it has been God's desire to dwell with His people in intimate fellowship—to know us and be known by us. I was a student at Grace University in

Omaha, Nebraska when I met her. She was an amazing woman of God and very humble. What struck me most was her ability to articulate to others what she understood of God's word. There were things she seemed understand about the Word that I didn't know you could understand. I attended church as a child, but it wasn't a regular or consistent part of my life. I came to Christ in a home Bible study in my 20s. I didn't feel attached to any particular denomination and had attended different types of churches over the years. When I entered Grace University, my first prayer would be the most significant one I prayed while there. It was simple, *"Lord, I am willing to have everything I think I know dismantled as long as I end up at Your truth."*

The next few years would revolutionize my walk with God and my understanding of His Word. Debbie was a fellow student. She was seasoned in the Word of God, and she and her husband led Bible study tours to Israel. As she spoke about her life and family, it was very clear she was intentional about the application of biblical truth to her daily living. After being in class with her for a while, I asked about her obvious love for and understanding of the Word. She mentioned a series of Bible studies she used in groups she met with regularly. My first study with her group was in the book of Romans—I was blown away and loved it. I quickly learned that God is willing to teach us the truth of His Word if we desire to be taught (1 John 2:27).

The more I read the Bible, the more aware I am of what I don't know as well as how awesome it is to get to know God more. I continue to read because I can always hear Him urging me on, *"So that you may know that I am God."* He beckons me to His heart with these words. They comfort me when I don't understand the *why* of something. He alone is God—sovereign, holy, righteous, just, loving, gracious, merciful and faithful. All of this is so that "I" may know that "He" is God!

Stay Humble

This counsel is from someone who has become a dear and beloved friend in very recent years. Her advice is simple—*stay humble.* It is both an encouragement and a warning to me. On the one hand, it is her way of communicating that she feels witness to God's potential in me. She believes in and recognizes His blessings on my life. At the same time, her advice is a gentle admonition that seeks to remind me, *they are His gifts . . . not mine.* It is *His* blessing. It is *His* anointing. I thank God for having friends like her in my life.

11

Tips for Ageless Beauty

N ear the end of his life, the apostle Paul declared, "I have fought the good fight . . . ." The life of a believer isn't a cakewalk. By design, it's laden with victories, trials, mountaintop and valley experiences. It may sometimes seem that seasons of trials in the valley outlast the victories or the mountain top experiences. Our character and potential for love are further refined in the fires of trial and tribulation. We're conformed to the image of Christ and sanctified by God's Word and His presence as we encounter people and situations that rub against our lives. Sometimes those *rubbing* (and often abrasive) experiences run counter to the direction we're headed. Yet they serve a critical purpose in our lives. These principles are intended to help us avoid bitterness of spirit, resentment, anger and despair as we journey.

Christ is enough

> See to it that no one takes you captive through philosophy and empty deception, according to the tradition of men, according to the elementary principles of the world, rather

than according to Christ. For in Him all the fullness of Deity dwells in bodily form, and in Him you have been made complete, and He is the head over all rule and authority. (Colossians 2:8-10 NASB)

A literal translation of Colossians 2:9 might read: *"In Christ is housed permanently the cramming of all of Who the Godhead is. And in Him, you've been crammed into, too."* This verse ranks high on my list of favorite Scripture passages. It's one of the most powerful statements in the Word. It makes a complex truth very simple. All of the fullness of the Godhead resides in Christ. *Because we are in Him and He is in us, we are complete.* We're crammed full of God, and the fact is He's bursting to get out and into our lives! It's a startling truth in light of how we live. Despite the fact that we're packed full God, we chase ambition for ambition's sake. We search for other things outside of ourselves to be complete. Our completeness, capacity, and destiny are fulfilled in Christ. There's no piece of *secret knowledge* lurking behind some *new idea* that will suddenly propel you into some *elusive destiny*—not apart from Christ. The apostle Paul takes great care to warn us not to be ensnared (e.g., trapped) by any concept, philosophy, or hoopla that would dupe us into believing we are less than sufficient in Christ. *He is our sufficiency!*

At some point, we must come to terms with this truth—*Christ is enough.* Nothing more is necessary and nothing less will do. One year, after celebrating Thanksgiving with my parents and siblings, I considered how blessed I feel whenever I spend time with them. It is always a refreshing and encouraging time for me. It's something I try not to take for granted, and I'm very grateful for it. As I made the trip home from Atlanta, I began asking myself this question:

"How much more does God have to do to prove He loves you?"

What is it that causes me to doubt His love for me? Every person in my life in every aspect of my history is a beautiful reminder of His love and faithfulness. Yet, I occasionally still struggle with whether I am *love-worthy*. I am sure there are those who would argue that all of us are *worthy of love* on some level. My conclusion is this: The issue isn't whether or not I am worthy of love. The issue is that God has, in fact, chosen to love me. He has proven it by sending His Son to lay down His life for me, investing Himself in me, and promising a future for me (John 3:16, Ephesians 1:13-14). He has made His home in my heart. I am a temple of His Holy Spirit, a habitation for His glory. He loves me. He loves me. He loves me! It is something I must remind myself of every day. You must remind yourself of this truth as well—every day! Christ is enough, and He loves and adores you! For today, let that be enough.

Stay focused

> Therefore if you have been raised up with Christ, keep seeking the things above, where Christ is, seated at the right hand of God. Set your mind on the things above, not on the things that are on earth. For you have died and your life is hidden with Christ in God. When Christ, who is our life, is revealed, then you also will be revealed with Him in glory. (Colossians 3:1-4 NASB)

The city of Colosse is representative of the challenges that face us when it comes to how our beauty is defined. Colosse was a metropolitan city and central hub for commerce and culture.[27] It was a small city with a mixed population of ethnicities and cultures. Because of its location along a trade route, it became a melting pot of ideas and philosophies as different cultures made their way through the region. As a result, Colosse's culture and social climate took on a very syncretistic persona.

Syncretism is *the incorporation into religious faith and practice of elements from other religions, resulting in a loss of integrity and assimilation to the surrounding culture.*[28] Christians in the region were encouraged to add *a little of this and a little of that* in order to *really* be complete and whole as believers. This trend explains Paul's admonition in Colossians 2:9 about their completeness in Christ and his further encouragement to not be taken captive by philosophy and empty deception.

Paul understood that if they bought into the lie that they weren't enough or needed *something extra* according the standard of the world (and its influences) around them, they would never experience all God had for them. They'd lose their focus amid a hodge-podge of junk and nonsense. His message is clear: *Stay focused on the One who saved you and is able to keep you.* We do this by first remembering that we were dead in our trespasses and sin. The only reason we live victoriously as believers is because we have been raised up with Christ. We should also keep seeking things above.

Endeavor to stay focused on what matters to God. Have a mindset that keeps all things *godly* as your priority. You already know this won't be easy. Daily responsibilities, work, church and even ministry obligations can cause us to lose our focus. *Sometimes life just gets in the way.* That, in fact, is the very reason we need to keep our minds on things above—life gets in the way. When it does, it can derail us if we're not careful.

We do have to be intentional and remind ourselves of how necessary this is for us to be effective and grow. We aren't the first who had to struggle to do *life*—even in a high technology age—and we won't be the last. I appreciate the fact that a man like Nehemiah was able to stay focused on his calling despite the distractions that surrounded him. As

Cupbearer to King Xerxes, he stayed focused after hearing the walls of Jerusalem were destroyed. He pondered, prayed and planned. Four months later, he emerged with a strategy for rebuilding the walls and leading the people (Nehemiah 1-2). His ability to stay focused increased his effectiveness as he moved forward and became a critical skill when persecution and rejection were mounting.

It may sometimes seem our day-to-day lives get in the way of our relationship with God. That perception is Satan's attempt to distort our purview. *This life* is where our sanctification process is worked out before the Lord. The real challenge is to narrow our attention to the One who matters most and those things that matter most to Him. Our *real life* is hidden in Him and our effectiveness and beauty are best showcased within the context of who He is.

Be steadfast and diligent

> . . . then Sanballat and Geshem sent a message to me, saying, "Come, let us meet together at Chephirim in the plain of Ono." But they were planning to harm me. So I sent messengers to them, saying, "I am doing a great work and I cannot come down. *Why should the work stop while I leave it and come down to you?"* They sent messages to me four times in this manner, and I answered them in the same way. (Nehemiah 6:2-4 NASB *emphasis mine*)

I love Nehemiah's response to Sanballat and Geshem. He was doing a great work and was resolute in his determination to not be pulled away from what God had placed in his heart. Nehemiah knew they meant to harm him, but he was *fixed* on finishing the work before him. A key secret for *ageless beauty* is to understand the value of remaining steadfast and being diligent to stay on task. As believers, we must be persistent to *stay on the wall.* Sanballat and Geshem are representative of the kinds of distractions that pull at us once we've decided to intentionally engage God.

Nehemiah had to refuse their requests four times and let them know he wasn't moving. Each request to meet was an attempt to intimidate him a little bit more. I love his question to them: *"Why should the work stop while I leave it and come down to you?"* Isn't that a great question? Why should the work stop for any of us? God has called us to be persistent in our pursuit of a greater understanding of who He is and deeper relationship with Him. *He is I AM.* There is no other like Him. He's waiting to draw near to us when we draw near to Him. Listen, it may not be enough to tell the Enemy to leave you alone one time. We must be diligent and resolute in our determination to go after God—to seek His face—to truly worship Him.

As in Nehemiah's case, there might be those who are watching and reporting on your deeds whether good or bad. Our goal must be to remain focused on the task at hand. The Enemy of our souls will be relentless in his efforts to disrupt the work God has given us. Those efforts may manifest through coworkers, neighbors, associates, friends, even family. Satan will resort to lies and distortions to pull you off task. His goal is to evoke fear, intimidation and irrational behavior. Sanballat and Tobiah had hoped to lure Nehemiah away in order to harm him. When their tactics did not succeed, they resorted to using lies and accusation. Their hope was to discourage all of the people through their persistence and to stop the work.

Sanballat and Tobiah were so desperate to discourage him they hired someone to lie to Nehemiah. Nehemiah wisely concluded they had hoped to make him so fearful that he would act irrationally and sin. There is a huge lesson for us here. Acting out of our fears can cause us to sin as well. Nehemiah had to be strategic and discerning regarding their attempts. In verse 9, he prays, " . . . now, Oh God, strengthen my hands." *The key to resiliency and steadfastness is intimacy with God.* Nehemiah did what he knew best—he prayed. He was able to be resilient and press through to the end. The wall was rebuilt in 52 days. When the surrounding nations heard what God had done, it caused them to lose their confidence in their ability to oppose the work.

Is prayer what you know best? Is it a primary weapon in your arsenal against attack? I'm working on it as I experience attacks in my own life. I must remind myself often not to come off the wall. What is your wall? Is it praying for your children, believing God for friend's salvation, or trusting Him for your healing? *Stay on the wall Beloved.* When fiery darts are flying from every direction, secure the shield of faith to you, keep wielding the sword of the spirit with the other hand, and shout, *"Why should the work stop while I leave it and come down to you!"*

> Therefore, my beloved brethren, be steadfast, immovable, always abounding in the work of the Lord, knowing that your toil is not in vain in the Lord. (1 Corinthians 15:58 NASB)

Remember who you are

Isn't it just like God to put us in the best win-win situation ever? He steps out of eternity into time to save us through His death on the cross. He then ensures our success by promising to never leave or abandon us (Hebrews 13:5). On top of all of that, He sends a Helper to comfort, guide, teach and correct us. Our God is awesome! Holy Spirit helps our weaknesses, searches our hearts and intercedes for us according to God's will (Romans 8:26-27). Frankly, He can't mess this up. We have a Helper! What a marvelous truth! No matter what happens, remember the new identity you have acquired in Christ. Let's run down the short list very quickly:

You are chosen!

But you are A CHOSEN RACE, A royal PRIESTHOOD,
A HOLY NATION, A PEOPLE FOR God's OWN
POSSESSION, so that you may proclaim the excellencies of
Him who has called you out of darkness into His marvelous
light; for you once were NOT A PEOPLE, but now you
are THE PEOPLE OF GOD; you had NOT RECEIVED
MERCY, but now you have RECEIVED MERCY. Beloved,
I urge you as aliens and strangers to abstain from fleshly
lusts which wage war against the soul. Keep your behavior
excellent among the Gentiles, so that in the thing in which
they slander you as evildoers, they may because of your
good deeds, as they observe them, glorify God in the day of
visitation. (1 Peter 2:9-12 NASB)

You are an overcomer!

Whoever believes that Jesus is the Christ is born of God,
and whoever loves the Father loves the child born of Him.
By this we know that we love the children of God, when we
love God and observe His commandments. For this is the
love of God, that we keep His commandments; and His
commandments are not burdensome. For whatever is born
of God overcomes the world; and this is the victory that has
overcome the world—our faith. (1 John 5:1-4 NASB)

You have God on your side!

If God is for us, who is against us? He who did not spare
His own Son, but delivered Him over for us all, how will He
not also with Him freely give us all things? Who will bring
a charge against God's elect? God is the one who justifies;

who is the one who condemns? Christ Jesus is He who died, yes, rather who was raised, who is at the right hand of God, who also intercedes for us. Who will separate us from the love of Christ? Will tribulation, or distress, or persecution, or famine, or nakedness, or peril, or sword? Just as it is written, "FOR YOUR SAKE WE ARE BEING PUT TO DEATH ALL DAY LONG; WE WERE CONSIDERED AS SHEEP TO BE SLAUGHTERED." But in all these things we overwhelmingly conquer through Him who loved us. For I am convinced that neither death, nor life, nor angels, nor principalities, nor things present, nor things to come, nor powers, nor height, nor depth, nor any other created thing, will be able to separate us from the love of God, which is in Christ Jesus our Lord. (Romans 8:28-39 NASB)

You have a Helper!

In the same way the Spirit also helps our weakness; for we do not know how to pray as we should, but the Spirit Himself intercedes for us with groanings too deep for words; and He who searches the hearts knows what the mind of the Spirit is, because He intercedes for the saints according to the will of God. (Romans 8:26-27 NASB)

Since we have these truths, may I encourage you (and me) to keep the faith? As I mentioned at the beginning of this chapter, the apostle Paul knew his time on earth was coming to an end. When he wrote to Pastor Timothy, he was able to reflect on the fact that he had done his best to be faithful to the call of God on his life. He wasn't anxious about his future, nor was he fretting about his past. He knew he had stood strong in the faith, and he had been obedient to do all God had instructed and commanded him to do. Paul was confident the future that lay before him was a glorious one. He knew who he was in Christ Jesus, and he knew he could trust the righteous Judge. You, too, can trust the righteous Judge—He's on your side!

> For I am already being poured out as a drink offering, and the time of my departure has come. I have fought the good fight, I have finished the course, I have kept the faith; in the future there is laid up for me the crown of righteousness, which the Lord, the righteous Judge, will award to me on that day; and not only to me, but also to all who have loved His appearing. (2 Timothy 4:6-8 NASB)

CONCLUSION

A Final Thought

Then Caleb quieted the people before Moses and said, "We should by all means go up and take possession of it, for we will surely overcome it." But the men who had gone up with him said, " We are not able to go up against the people, for they are too strong for us." So they gave out to the sons of Israel a bad report of the land which they had spied out, saying, "The land through which we have gone, in spying it out, is *a land that devours its inhabitants*; and all the people whom we saw in it are *men of great size.* "There also we saw the Nephilim (the sons of Anak are part of the Nephilim); and *we became like grasshoppers in our own sight, and so we were in their sight.*" (Numbers 13:30-33 NASB *emphasis mine*)

One of the problems with the 10 spies was they allowed themselves to be overwhelmed by everything they saw around them. They saw a land that devoured its inhabitants. They saw men of great size. Yet their greatest problem seemed to be *they were diminishing the size of their own God.* I wonder if it is an affront to God when we believe our problem is too great a challenge for Him? This account in Scripture always arrests my attention. It is easy to assess the response of the 10 spies and highlight their shortcomings and lack of faith. Their perspective cost them dearly. They would die in the wilderness and never see the Promised Land. It was all because they could not see with spiritual eyes. I know that experience—I think many of us do. For as much faith as I think I have, I sometimes let the size of the giants distort my vision as well.

At first glance, it would appear this was the error of the 10 spies. It was true—there were giants, and they had devoured the land. That, however, should have been the least of their worries. The greater threats were *the giants within them—the giants of fear, unbelief and hardness of heart.* They allowed these *internal security threats* to conquer them before giants in the land were able to get near them. They refused to believe God was who He said He was. Their *grasshopper thinking* was a consequence of their unbelief (Hebrews 4:1-12). Their refusal to put their full assurance in God made their hearts hard, produced the fruit of unbelief and secured the judgment of not entering the Promised Land.

Joshua and Caleb never denied the vastness of the land or its ability to devour its inhabitants. They never denied the great size of the men in the land. They, too, saw there were giants in the land. Despite this they were able to look at the situation and compare it to the *bigness* of their God. How they perceived what they saw was directly related to the pliability of their heart and their faith in God. In doing so, they refused to see themselves as grasshoppers and shrink back in fear.

I cannot tell you if Joshua and Caleb perceived themselves as greater giants than the men in the land. What is evident, however, is they knew they could take possession of the land and overcome it. They understood their capacity to do so had nothing to do with giants or grasshoppers. Their capacity to take the land was related to a willingness to fully follow God (Numbers 14:24). If they were following God, it would not matter who or what they encountered. Don't be dismayed if you feel the need to preach that short exhortation to yourself weekly! I do it all of the time. When Giants show up and when the land seems too vast, I have to remind myself those things do not matter. What does matter is what I know about my heavenly Father. What does matter is what I believe about the integrity of His heart and the promises He has made to us as His children.

God is willing and able to slay giants for us! He says to us don't be dismayed—*don't allow yourselves to be shattered or confounded by your history, by your present, by your wounds or your scars.* If we shrink and become grasshoppers in our own sight—if hardness of heart and a refusal to believe God usurp our faith—we will certainly shrink in the sight of others especially the Devil. *Don't shrink back! You're no grasshopper. God has made you beautiful, strong, valiant and courageous!* He has equipped you with everything you need for living a whole and godly life. *Now, go live like it Beautiful!*

PARTICIPANT'S GUIDE

Part I—He Makes All Things Beautiful
by Healing Our Wounds

1. In 2 Corinthians 10:12, the apostle Paul warns that we shouldn't compare ourselves among ourselves (this would include siblings, friends, co-workers, etc.) because it is unwise. How have your own comparisons of yourself to others caused damaging wounds (emotional, spiritual, mental) in your life?

2. Reflect on Psalm 139:14-15. What insights do you gather from this passage that may be a source of encouragement to you when there is the tendency to compare yourself to someone else?

3. King Saul appeared to have had a real problem with the praise David received as it compared with the praise he received. He was unable to *manage the perceptions* of what the people thought of him in light of David's reputation. What are the potential dangers when we find it more important to manage the perceptions people have of us (or others) rather than focus on God's will for our lives?

4. Reflect on a time when you've been offended because you felt unappreciated or overlooked. How did remembering God's promises (whether you read the Word or were reminded by a friend) help redirect your thoughts and change your behavior?

5. Describe an area of your life where you need to "uproot offense." What steps can you take to begin to deal with the damaged emotions that have resulted from offense?

Part 2—He Makes All Things Beautiful by Invading Our World

1. How has God invaded your world?

2. As you examine each of these accounts from history, what characteristic(s) of God's nature do you observe? How can remembering that aspect of His character encourage you?

3. How does Rahab's story encourage you in your relationship with God? How does it increase your understanding of His nature?

4. How significant is it that Rahab is listed in the lineage of Christ in Matthew 1:5? How could you encourage others with this fact?

5. Describe how His name, Immanuel (God with us), speaks to and encourages you?

6. What has your response to God's invasion of your world been like? How have you embraced an understanding of who He is?

7. The Shunammite Woman was able to declare, "All is well," despite the gravity of her situation. Consider your current circumstances/ situation. How can you embrace an *"All is well"* perspective?

8. Describe how an *"It's never like you imagine it"* mindset has impacted your life or dreams?

9. Describe how an inaccurate perception of the nature and character of God can impact your relationship with Him? . . . with others?

10. What does it mean for *you* to fully engage the life God has granted you? In what ways are you "pushing back" against it?

Part 3—He Makes All Things Beautiful by Giving Us Beauty Secrets for Life

1. Which aspects of each beauty regimen present the greatest challenge(s) for you? Why?
   - Cleanse deeply

   - Refine and tone

   - Moisturize

   - Ageless beauty

2. What personal beauty secrets have been important in your life?

ABOUT THE AUTHOR

Marvita Franklin

Marvita was born in Bethesda, Maryland and was raised in Atlanta, Georgia. She graduated from Francis Howell High School in St. Charles, Missouri and attended Brown's Business and Secretarial College in St. Louis to study Accounting following her graduation.

She began her U. S. Air Force career in 1981 and retired in 2001. She has over 25 years of progressive leadership experience and responsibility in the Air Force and civil service. She has served as the Director of Education to oversee programs of instruction and curriculum development for leadership, management and communicative skills courses for two levels of Professional Military Education within the Air Force. She has also served as Assistant Airport Manager for military airfields in the United States, Europe and the Middle East. In recent years, she has served as a Leadership Coach and Trainer within the U.S. Army Recruiting Command. In that role, she provided training on cognitive and human factors which impact leader performance and provided behavioral performance coaching for Army recruiters.

Her education includes a Masters Degree in Human Resource Development from Clemson University, Clemson SC; a Bachelor of

Science Degree with a double major in Biblical Studies and Management & Organizational Leadership from Grace University, Omaha, NE; and an Associate of Applied Science Degree in Instructor Technology from the Community College of the Air Force.

Marvita is a Sunday school teacher and sings in her church choir. She has a passion for teaching God's Word and helping to develop seasoned and emerging leaders. Her life mission statement is, "To make God's Word plain and practical so His people live victoriously." She has been a Children's Choir Director, Christian Education Coordinator, Precept Bible Study Facilitator and a Small Group Leader.

She is married and has two children. She loves reading, journaling and writing. In her spare time, she loves to scrapbook, sew and do anything else "craft-related."

EMAIL: vita@marvitafranklin.com
BLOG: http://www.marvitafranklin.com
TWITTER: http://twitter.com/MarvitaFranklin
FACEBOOK: http://facebook.com/AVictoriousView

NOTES

Part I—He makes all things beautiful by healing our wounds

Zodhiates, Spiros. *The Complete Word Study Dictionary: New Testament*. electronic ed. Chattanooga, TN: AMG Publishers, 2000.

Chapter I—The source of our wounds

AHCPR Publication No. 95-0654, Treating Pressure Sores, Dec 1994 . . .

AHCPR Publication No. 95-0654, Treating Pressure Sores, Dec 1994 . . .

Baker, Warren, and Eugene E. Carpenter. *The Complete Word Study Dictionary: Old Testament*. Chattanooga, TN: AMG Publishers, 2003.

Zodhiates, Spiros. *The Complete Word Study Dictionary: New Testament*. electronic ed. Chattanooga, TN: AMG Publishers, 2000.

The Holy Bible: Holman Christian Standard Version., Lk 7:22-23 (Nashville: Holman Bible Publishers, 2009).

The Holy Bible: New International Version, Mt 13:53-58 (Grand Rapids, MI: Zondervan, 1984).

The Holy Bible: English Standard Version, Jn 6:60-61 (Wheaton: Standard Bible Society, 2001).

9   *skandalízō*; fut. *skandalísō*, a trap, stumbling block.
    Zodhiates, Spiros. *The Complete Word Study Dictionary: New Testament*. electronic ed. Chattanooga, TN: AMG Publishers, 2000.

10 *skándalon*; gen. *skandálou*, neut. noun. The trigger of a trap on which the bait is placed, and which, when touched by the animal, springs and causes it to close causing entrapment.
    Zodhiates, Spiros. *The Complete Word Study Dictionary: New Testament*. electronic ed. Chattanooga, TN: AMG Publishers, 2000.

11 **tap•root** \-ˌrüt, -ˌru̇t\ *noun* **1:** a primary root that grows vertically downward and gives off small lateral roots; **2:** the central element or position in a line of growth or development.
    Merriam-Webster, Inc. *Merriam-Webster's Collegiate Dictionary*. Eleventh ed. Springfield, MA: Merriam-Webster, Inc., 2003.

12 Patterson, Kerry; Grenny, Joseph; McMillan, Ron; Switzler, Al. *Crucial Conversations: Tools for Talking When Stakes are High, Pg 99,* McGraw Hill New York, NY, 2002

Chapter 2—When offense takes root

13 Patterson, Kerry; Grenny, Joseph; McMillan, Ron; Switzler, Al. *Crucial Conversations: Tools for Talking When Stakes are High, Pg 99,* McGraw Hill New York, NY, 2002

14 Genesis 9

15 Patterson, Kerry et al, Crucial Confrontations

Chapter 5—God's invasion of their world

16 This is a reference from a book titled, The Miracle of the Scarlet Thread by Richard Booker, Destiny Image Publishers, 1981

Part 3—He makes all things beautiful by giving us beauty secrets for life

[17] Hoodwinked (™), The Weinstein Company, 2005

[18] Zodhiates, Spiros. *The Complete Word Study Dictionary: New Testament*. electronic ed. Chattanooga, TN: AMG Publishers, 2000.

Chapter 7—Cleanse deeply

[19] Baker, Warren, and Eugene E. Carpenter. *The Complete Word Study Dictionary: Old Testament*. Chattanooga, TN: AMG Publishers, 2003.

[20] Zodhiates, Spiros. *The Complete Word Study Dictionary: New Testament*. electronic ed. Chattanooga, TN: AMG Publishers, 2000.

Chapter 9—Moisturize

[21] sklerodardia (greek 4641); hard-heartedness, destitution of spiritual perception.

[22] Merriam-Webster, Inc. *Merriam-Webster's Collegiate Dictionary*. Eleventh ed. Springfield, MA: Merriam-Webster, Inc., 2003.

[23] Zodhiates, Spiros. *The Complete Word Study Dictionary: New Testament*. electronic ed. Chattanooga, TN: AMG Publishers, 2000.

[24] Peterson, Eugene H. *A Long Obedience in the Same Direction*. Downers Grove, IL: InterVarsity Press, 1980.

Chapter 10—Personal Beauty Secrets

[25] Emphasis mine.

[26] Zodhiates, Spiros. *The Complete Word Study Dictionary: New Testament*. electronic ed. Chattanooga, TN: AMG Publishers, 2000.

Chapter 11—Tips for Ageless Beauty

[27] Dockery, David S., Trent C. Butler, Christopher L. Church et al. *Holman Bible Handbook*. Nashville, TN: Holman Bible Publishers, 1992.

[28] Martin H. Manser, *Dictionary of Bible Themes: The Accessible and Comprehensive Tool for Topical Studies* (London: Martin Manser, 1999).